My Name's not Susie

My Name's not Susie

A Life Transformed by Literacy

Sharon Jean Hamilton

Foreword by Janice Lauer

Boynton/Cook Publishers
Heinemann
Portsmouth, NH

Boynton/Cook Publishers, Inc.
A subsidiary of Reed Elsevier Inc.
361 Hanover Street
Portsmouth, NH 03801-3912

Offices and agents throughout the world

We would like to thank those who have given their permission to include material in this book.
Every effort has been made to contact the copyright holders for permission to reprint borrowed
material where necessary. We regret any oversights that may have occurred and would be happy
to rectify them in future printings of this work.

Excerpt from "East Coker" in FOUR QUARTETS, copyright © 1943 by T.S. Eliot and renewed
1971 by Esme Valerie Eliot, reprinted by permission of Harcourt Brace & Company and Faber and
Faber Ltd.

Excerpts from ON BEING LITERATE by Margaret Meek, published by The Bodley Head. Copyright
© 1991 by Margaret Meek. Reprinted by permission of Random House UK Ltd. and
Heinemann, A division of Reed Elsevier Inc., Portsmouth, NH.

Excerpt from "The Love Song of J. Alfred Prufrock" by T.S. Eliot. Reprinted by permission of
Harcourt Brace & Company.

"A Day in the Life of a Winnipeg Research Student in London" by Sharon J. Hamilton originally
appeared in the *MTS Update*, 1985. Reprinted by permission of the Manitoba Teachers' Society.

Excerpts from MAJOR MODERN ESSAYISTS 2/E by Gilbert Muller. Copyright © 1994. Reprinted
by permission of Prentice Hall Inc.

Excerpt from "An Elementary School Classroom in a Slum" from SELECTED POEMS by Stephen
Spender. Copyright © 1942 and renewed 1970 by Stephen Spender. Reprinted by permission
of Random House, Inc.

Library of Congress Cataloging-in-Publication Data
Hamilton, Sharon J.
    My name's not Susie : a life transformed by literacy / Sharon Jean
Hamilton.
        p. cm.
    ISBN 0-86709-361-7
    1. Hamilton, Sharon J.   2. English teachers—Indiana—
Indianapolis—Biography.   3. Socially handicapped children—
Education—Canada—Case studies.   4. Children—Canada—Books and
reading.   5. Literacy.   I. Title.
PE64.H36A3   1995
82.9—dc20
[B]   95-18077
                                                                         CIP

Editor: Peter Stillman
Production: Renée Le Verrier
Cover design: Gwen Frankfeldt
Cover photo: Courtesy of Winnipeg Children's Aid Society

Printed in the United States of America on acid-free paper
98 97 96   VB   2 3 4 5 6

For Katherine Aird Hamilton

Contents

Acknowledgments

WRITING THIS BOOK HAS NOT BEEN A SOLITARY ENTERPRISE. Friends and colleagues around the world have been willing to read and comment on the manuscript as it has moved through its many drafts. For their encouragement, extensive commentary, and helpful suggestions, I am most indebted to Deb Agard, Jeanne Gerlach, Janice Lauer, Robert Orr, and Nancy Thompson in the United States, to Glenys Acland, Bernice Brown, Olga Kruk, and Mary Maguire in Canada, to John Dixon, Jean Dunning, and Harold Rosen in England, and to Mary Mannison in Australia.

Since memory assumes such a significant role in this manuscript, I am indebted to my mother, Katherine Aird Hamilton; my son, Deejay (David) Dayton; and my birth father, Jack Fleming for verifying the accuracy of family-related information.

For providing the catalyst to begin, I thank the students in my writing classes, whose developing relationship with literacy focused my approach and shaped the meaning that this manuscript has given to my life. In particular, I thank Stephanie Rodriguez and Ann Nicholas, whose contributions in the Epilogue demonstrate the extent to which our interactions with literacy influence our interactions with life.

Making meaning from experience requires selecting a particular lens to focus on a still point in the swirling chaos of existence. I thank Margaret Meek, of the University of London Institute of Education, and her book *On Being Literate* (Heinemann, 1992), for many of the ideas that brought a focus to what might otherwise have been meandering explorations or retellings of experience.

Even with computers, wrestling a manuscript into publishable form is a challenge. I thank Marsha Neawedde for her patience in reformatting the entire text and making the seemingly endless revisions during the final stages of preparing the manuscript for the publishers.

Foreword

EVERY DAY WE HEAR STORIES OF CHILDREN BEING ABUSED OR IN-
juring others. We listen to accounts of families that live in poverty one
generation after another. In the face of such apparent inevitability, this book
presents a heartening countertale, a record of the power of literacy and
compassion for one desolate child. This narrative allows us to trace the
transformation of this lost child, to follow her down the paths that reading
and writing opened, and ultimately to rejoice in her accomplishments.

Fittingly, Sharon Hamilton has framed her story as a literacy narrative,
a genre being used today by scholars to recount the ways in which reading
and writing construct the ideas, beliefs, and values of a community and its
members. In this story, we watch a little girl break out of her isolation into
a family; we witness her imagination soaring to magical places; and we see
her discovering new views of herself as she meets the naughty princess, the
ugly duckling, and Anne of Green Gables. Later we observe her in London
as she realizes through Proust that she is authoring her life, choosing some
memories and forgetting others, and as she ponders the Proustian idea that
she is the sum of everyone's reactions to her.

Told with the courage that risks the loss of privacy, this story resonates
with the author's remembrances, painful at times, of her growing sense of
values and her escape from the narrow world of fear and hopelessness into
which she had been plunged. Sharon brings to her own story a retrospective
understanding of the ways that literacy shapes a person, a theoretical perspective that enriches but never interrupts the sequence of events. Her documen-
tation is subtle as she mentions records of the Children's Aid Society, her
mother's accounts, or her childhood writings. Now, as a university professor,
she is motivated to explore her painful past to encourage her students, who

also struggle to make sense of their difficult experiences and who have come to higher education, to her, for better lives. Sharon generously offers herself to them as an exemplar but also engages them in her search for meaning, drawing them into collaboration as she writes her life.

The narrative has both an immediacy and a distance. Sharon as theorist remains in the background, allowing the reader to enter the story and experience the terrors and joys of this child who eventually enters the University of London, but she is never far behind, selecting and interpreting these life events. Unlike the ethnographer who recounts the literacy events of others, Sharon is both scholar and subject, the teller and the told, constructing her conflicted selves in the process.

More than Sharon Hamilton's story, this book is a record of the generosity of a couple who were willing to take into their home the "worst" child at the Children's Aid Society. We learn of their patience with her wild behavior and fears, their wise sayings, their gentle discipline, their gift of stories and books. We also meet their limitations as seen through the eyes of a child who found herself always second to their "natural" son. Yet this exceptional mother, now in her nineties, has allowed the tale to be told.

As the story progresses, we gradually realize that literacy is a two-edged sword. It opens doors to higher education, to a rewarding life of teaching. At the same time, it generates increasing tension between husband and wife, within families, and between friends, as gender roles are unmasked in their grimness and as alternative lifestyles are highlighted through literature and theory. Unlike most of her blood brothers and sisters (discovered later), who have lived within a limited radius of Winnipeg and found little or no joy in schooling, Sharon has risked much for literacy in her adult life, leaving one seemingly comfortable place after another: the nurture of a friend, a rewarding position as a high school department chair, life with her son, and the familiarity of her country. Fascinated by the written word, she has followed the leads of literacy from Canada to England to the United States.

One leaves this book with an impression of the rich symbolic pattern that marks Sharon Hamilton's adult life as she continues to fashion herself through drama, dance, discourse, and music. The various personae of the author, Karen, Sharon, and Susie, are never fully coherent or reconciled but rather remain caught up in the literacy process, which, as Paulo Friere says, transforms even as it constructs reality.

Janice Lauer
Purdue University

The Literacy Narrative

WHAT AND WHY

LITERACY SALVAGED MY LIFE. IT IS AS SIMPLE AND FUNDAMENTAL as that. At the age of three and a half, I snuggled into a new mother's arms to be read to for the first time. That day I entered a world of princesses and pirates and gods and goddesses and little engines that could and little boys who called *wolf* once too often. This literary world, like my real world, was paradoxically predictable and unpredictable, safe and dangerous, ethical and deceptive, delightful and tragic, but in stories—at least the stories my new mother read to me every day from the first day she adopted me until I could read by myself—there was always a way to figure out what went wrong and why. My own life was not so easy to figure out.

When I was eight, in order to silence my constant talking for a few minutes, my mother suggested I write what I could remember about my early years of eighteen moves from foster home to foster home and then to the Greenhouse (my name for the "orphanage," or Children's Aid Society Receiving Home). Whenever reliving these early horrors upset me, my mother pointed out that the troubles I was writing about paled in comparison to the troubles of people I was reading about. I may have been unwanted, malnourished, and beaten, but I didn't starve or freeze to death like the little match girl, I wasn't forced to steal like Oliver Twist, I wasn't ever burned at a stake, buried alive, or thrown into the sea to drown. Writing about my life offered me a necessary perspective, but it took my mother, initially, to provide that perspective by emphasizing the differences between the drama of literature and what, by implication, were the lesser dramas of my life. It was a whole new lesson for me to learn much later that the dramas of our lives can be as soul-searing and soul-shaping as the great dramas of literature.

As a teacher in the public school system for seventeen years and as a professor of English for eight years, my professional life has been immersed in literacy development, my students' and my own. As a teacher of writing, I am granted privileged access not just to developing thought processes but also to the very heartbeats of my students' lives. I have met through their writing students so lost in their own pain that they can find no way out. I have met through their writing students so far out of touch with their own thoughts and feelings that they can find no way in.

Reading and writing provided both a way out of my own misery and a way into understanding the sources of that misery. At first, literacy provided escape from the real world, where there seemed to be no place for me, into a fantasy world of love and adventure. However, as I kept reading and writing, I learned a very different kind of escape. Literacy equipped me with the knowledge and confidence to decide how I would live my life as the kind of person I wanted to be. We hear a lot about the importance of literacy, primarily in functional terms of day-to-day living and preparation for the world of work. Those roles are undeniable. But literacy also plays a powerful role in the interior working-out of who we are and how we decide what will be the conduct of our day-to-day lives. That is the function of literacy this narrative explores.

My Name's not Susie

Indianapolis, 1992

THEY COME TO A WORLD WHERE INCREASE IN LITERACY OFFERS promise and hope for a better life. They come from home, from work, from families, from worlds they want to understand more fully or worlds they want to escape. The cramped classroom accepts its continuous ebb and flow of students with the seeming neutrality of shadowless fluorescence. By five forty-five in the evening they arrive exhausted from the day's demands, sinking tiredly one by one into the haphazard circle of desks. Their energy sinks with them until someone—sometimes it's me, sometimes a fellow student—galvanizes them to discuss a common concern.

Tonight it's Angie, who arrives with an announcement and an invitation. "Dr. Hamilton, I'm having a party on Saturday night to celebrate my divorce. Will you come? And you come too, Stephanie. And you, John. And you and you. All of you. You've all been so encouraging the past few weeks while I've been writing myself through this mess."

"This mess" is the process of escaping her brutal husband, source of the still visible bruises on her face and even more poignant bruises on her soul, evident in every one of the essays and journals she has written this semester.

"I'd love to, Angie," I reply, "but I've already made arrangements for Saturday night. I'm going out for dinner and then to the symphony."

"Dinner and the symphony?" echoes Stephanie. "Out for dinner and then to the symphony," she repeats slowly, as though tasting each word. "I know there are people who go out for dinner and to the symphony, but I've never actually known anyone who does that. I wonder what it would be like."

The gap between who we are and who we wish to be, between how

1

we live and how we want to live, is always there, sometimes a crack, sometimes a chasm. Crossing it is a ceaseless human challenge. Those who make the attempt choose from an array of means, depending upon how they perceive and define the nature of the gap. Some define it in terms of happiness, or money, or power, or love. All the students in this class, though very different one from another, share one common determination: they have all decided that education, specifically a literacy-based liberal arts education, will be their means of crossing the gap.

Stephanie's first essay in this class described living for two days in the New York City subway with three children, one still a tiny baby, escaping from the beatings with the fishing rod her husband had used on her and on their children. A later essay anguished over too violently smashing a cockroach crawling across her mirror, and explored the sources of that violence. Stephanie, Angie, and all the other student writers in this class are learning that they have a story to tell, and that telling it may become an impetus to some sort of understanding, insight, and even action.

They are all trying, in their writing in particular, and in their pursuit of higher education in general, to reach across their respective gaps to a different, better life. Given the option to call me Sharon or Dr. Hamilton, most of them choose Dr. Hamilton and utter it with definite respect, sometimes even with a kind of awe, not of me, whom they meet only one evening a week for four months and therefore scarcely know, but for the educational level the title proclaims, and for the life and background it implies.

The gap between who we are and who we wish to be. I look at Stephanie, slim, brown-eyed, beautiful, amazingly serene despite her chilling explorations of her life. I want to tell her that if she desires a life that includes going out for dinner and to the symphony, she can create it. I want to tell Angie that my spirit will be with her at her party even though I will be elsewhere. I want to tell them both that I know from my own experience the challenges and pitfalls of constructing a whole new definition and articulation of self through education, through reading about the lives of others and writing about one's own. But the moment to speak of these things passes, and they're left unsaid.

They aren't said, but they whirl through my thoughts as I drive to my home on Oceanline Drive. Oceanline Drive in the middle of landlocked Indianapolis? It was partly because of the address that I chose this home. It seemed a metaphor for the falseness of my own position.

The imposter syndrome—the feeling that one's ability is not sufficient to warrant one's position—is common, particularly among women. But for a long time I thought I was alone in my feelings of "fooling" others and even myself (when I occasionally felt I actually belonged among the professoriate). This uneasy sensation of falseness involved literacy, by which I mean the kind of literate behavior expected and practiced in the milieu toward which I had aspired and amazingly found myself in. I listened to my colleagues speak with relaxed intimacy of bodies of knowledge I had not yet encountered. I observed the casual grace of their manners of discourse, alert to nuances of how to agree and disagree while maintaining a friendly discussion. I heard colleagues take a strong stance different from the rest and defend it with confidence and intellectual passion. And I felt baffled at how I had come to be among them. I was fearful—as many of my students must be when they feel outside the literate behavior of the academy or of any other community they wish to be a part of—that at any moment I might say something absolutely stupid and "reveal" myself.

Myself.

At this moment of writing, I feel suddenly alone on a huge stage, facing a full audience who've paid their admission and are expecting something for their money, some moment of truth, some sudden insight or shock of self-knowledge to be gained from what I have to tell. I remember as a child panicking about performing at piano and dance recitals and being told, "You are the master of your art. You know more of what you are doing than anyone in the audience." Another bit of deception that even as a child I only half believed; I am still learning to be master of what I do and say.

I arrive home to find my answering machine blinking. "Dr. Hamilton, it's Ann. Ann Nicholas. I'm in the hospital. If you don't get home too late, could you please call me?" I recall Ann Nicholas in my evening writing class three years ago, breezy, blonde, and blowzy in short, tight skirts, leopard skin jacket, four-inch heels, and low self-esteem, wretched because her ex-husband had been awarded custody of Leisa, their eight-year-old daughter, and determined to gain control of her life through increased education. Last year Ann was in my Secondary English methods class, warm and intellectually enthusiastic, excited about her job as manager of a small local cinema, enjoying custody of eleven-year-old Leisa, and looking forward to beginning her teaching career the following year. I dial the number she has left and hear Ann's slightly slurred response. Multiple sclerosis. In response to my concern, she says, "But it's better than the alternative. At first they feared I had an inoperable brain tumor. MS is controllable, and I should still be able to teach. I learned from you to look not at what is pushing me down but at what is available to pull me up. As you said in class, 'It's a matter of perspective, of attitude.' That's why I wanted to talk with you."

As I hang up the phone, I feel awed by how Ann has made a few words from me the basis for an attitude that could sustain her through this crisis. And just as Ann attributed her perspective, at least in part, to me, I try to piece together the sources that shaped this viewpoint in my own mind. Among them are *The Power of Positive Thinking*, which my mother gave me in my early teens; my high school study of Hamlet—"There is nothing either good or bad but thinking makes it so"; a cutesy poster—"When life gives you lemons, make lemonade"; an art or science class where we looked at a picture of a woman, old or young depending on whether we focused on foreground or background, and learned about half empty/half full; and the tricky illusions in the art of Escher. Those snippets of literacy-laced experiences had somehow been woven into a fundamental pattern in my philosophy, a pattern of choosing to seek out the positive in situations that confront, challenge, and confound.

In tracing just this one strand of literacy events, I acknowledge the difficulty of talking about literacy in any kind of direct, empirical manner. That my understanding of self and of others was enhanced in almost a step-by-step fashion is undeniable; that my behavior eventually changed is equally evident to me and to others who know me; that a particular perspective or lens for viewing life events evolved bit by bit over time is also apparent. And yet the connecting threads between event and awareness and change are so entangled with other events and other circumstances that any assumption of literacy-based causation and connection is admittedly tenuous and arguable. Does my articulation of the pattern combine thought and memory with language to *create* the connections, or does language combine with thought and memory to *discover* the connections? And suddenly, as I pondered my own links between literacy events and personal growth, I connected what I was thinking with what my students had been doing in their writing.

Moments when insight couples with action are rare; the moments following my conversation with Ann, brimful of the horrors and challenges of my students' lives, crystallized into a commitment. Having negotiated a way through my own horrors and challenges primarily with the help of education and educators, having become an educator myself, capable at times of helping others confront and conquer their individual horrors and challenges, I might possibly be able to help even more. Perhaps I could wipe away, in text, the veneer of my success that conceals the scars of abuse, neglect, self-doubt, and self-destructive, potentially criminal behavior. Perhaps I could show the sad, maladjusted child discovering how literacy could enable her to create a better life. I could delineate connections between reading and thinking about the lives of others and crossing the chasm from the life I found myself in to the life I wanted. Having been branded a borderline autistic, a potential sociopath, a bad apple unlikely ever to finish school or hold a job—all before I was three years old—I could perhaps show the dangers of labeling kids too early. Having flirted dangerously with criminal behavior in my late teens while dancing in a night club that fronted for a prostitution ring, I could perhaps show how sharp is the razor's edge that separates socially acceptable from socially deviant behavior, and how a wounded soul can so easily bleed from one into the other. I could perhaps show how literacy—how being read to and then learning to read and write— helped me to envision worlds beyond my miserable world and eventually enabled me to recreate my life as the kind of life I wanted.

Tonight, after having started to write this story at least a dozen times in earlier years and giving it up as seeming self-indulgence, I vow to put my experiences of crossing the chasm to better use. This literacy narrative is the result of that vow.

For Ann, for Angie, and for Stephanie, for all my student writers who are reaching across the chasm, for all who fear remaining imprisoned by circumstance, who have been confined by labels and categories, for myself, I tell this story.

1

Assaulting the Inarticulate

WINNIPEG, 1944

So here I am, in the middle way, having had . . . [fifty] years—

. . . . .

Trying to learn to use words, and every attempt

Is a wholly new start, and a different kind of failure

Because one has only learnt to get the better of words

For the thing one no longer has to say, or the way in which

One is no longer disposed to say it. And so each venture

Is a new beginning, a raid on the inarticulate . . .

—T. S. Eliot, *"East Coker"*

This story is indeed a raid, a verbal assault on the inarticulate. The tools of literacy—words—scratch at the surface of meaning differently from day to day. Words of fury and rage may claw at a memory one day; words of compassion and insight may soothe that same memory another day. The events of literacy are almost invisible, imprecise. Do we remember the exact moment we could read? The exact moment we could write? The exact moment we realized that what has been written, by ourselves or by someone else, is only one version of truth and sometimes a blatant lie? an incomplete or even false interpretation

7

of the chaos of existence? This opening chapter initiates my verbal raid on the inarticulate even as it describes societal and domestic assault on an inarticulate child.

I WAS NAMED KAREN AGNES FLEMING, THE SECOND CHILD OF Irene Fleming, still a child herself at nineteen, and the first to be fathered by her husband, Jack Fleming. This is Karen's story. But it is also Sharon's, and Susie's, and Floozie's, and Cooties', and even Gravel Gertie's story. It is a story of using literacy to live beyond the labels that create boundaries and limit dreams and possibilities.

I was born July 1, 1944. I can state that as a fact because my birth certificate says so. Actually, my birth certificate, which I didn't see until I was eighteen, says that is when Sharon Jean Hamilton was born, showing that even the documented facts of who is born and when are open to question. At age nine, suspecting for a myriad of reasons that I might be a pixie child brought to life by magic, I tried to locate my birth announcement, but I found no proclamation or verification of my entry into the world either as Karen Agnes Fleming or as Sharon Jean Hamilton. Until age sixteen, when I finally saw the certificate of adoption bearing both my names, my birth was far from a fact. Empirical evidence of my physical being notwithstanding, having no written-down textual evidence of my entry on earth, I questioned whether I was truly a human entity.

That Irene and Jack Fleming were my biological parents is also stated as fact, but these are facts that I had no access to while I was growing up. At age forty-two, having just returned to Winnipeg from three years of doctoral study in England, I learned that I had nine siblings, eight younger and one older, all born to a woman named Irene Fleming, née Lawrence, all still alive and having grown up within a fifteen-mile radius of one another. I also learned that Jack Fleming, my birth father, was alive and living in Calgary, and had fathered another daughter, making the total number of my new siblings ten. Additionally, I learned that my birth mother, Irene Fleming, had died in 1971 at the age of forty-six. The story of how all these discoveries came about will be told as the narrative continues, but the fact of these discoveries is essential here for explaining how I came to know and am able to recount events in my life that I could not possibly have remembered. As the last cog to be put into place in this recently discovered family wheel, I was informed in 1986 that my records at the Children's Aid Society, according to the Freedom of Information Act, would be available to me. I arranged for an appointment to view these records and embarked upon an astounding journey back through my early years.

AUGUST 18, 1986, WINNIPEG, CHILDREN'S AID SOCIETY ON EDmonton Street. I wait comfortably for my appointment, proud of my newly acquired doctorate in language and literature from London University, confident that what I have achieved so far in my life will more than make up for anything I might discover in these records. Almost fifteen minutes late, a distraught social worker introduces herself to me with the following words: "On behalf of the Children's Aid Society, I am so sorry." Her apology seems excessive for the brief wait, but she continues, "We have reviewed your file [at that very instant I realize that *file* and *life* have identical letters] and have decided that it would not be in your best interest for you to read it yourself. Instead, I have selected parts of it, the parts that we think you will be most interested in, and I will read those parts aloud to you [these *I*'s and *we*'s whirl through my mind too quickly to be challenged]. You can, of course, take notes as I read, and stop me to ask questions. If I can give you any further information, I will."

Why do I acquiesce? Why do I not contest this arbitrary decision? Partly because I hate contention and avoid it whenever I can, but mostly because I fear whatever has caused that distressed look still hovering in her eyes. If someone has determined that I am better off not knowing what is in those records, there must be good reason.

What was told at that meeting is described in the following pages, fleshed out with the help of correspondence and conversation with Jack Fleming, my birth father, whom I contacted, after much thought and reservation, in 1990, four years later.

FROM ALL I HAVE BEEN TOLD, I WAS ONE OF THOSE RARE BABIES born "bad." I stormed my way colicky and crotchety into a family already clouded by Jack's recent realization that Jackie, my elder sister, was not his child. Irene had deceived Jack Fleming into marrying her by convincing him that she was pregnant with his child. Jack, the bemused groom, had been—as he told me when I located him more than forty years later— "no match for the streetwise, flirtatious Irene," who at seventeen was already familiar with the dark habits of the dark alleys in the North End of Winnipeg.

Right from my birth I seemed to have continual confirmation that I was bad. I write *seemed to have* because, of course, I cannot remember any of this. What I can recall is that from my earliest memories until I was almost thirty, I saw myself mirrored in others' reactions to me as bad and considered it one of my main challenges in life to overcome this intrinsic badness. Not until I studied psychology did I begin to realize that, wanting to be good, I could not possibly have been intrinsically bad. Not until I encountered Edmund in *King Lear* and Iago in *Othello* did I begin to investigate on a literary plane the psychology of villainy, of badness, and determine that I really was otherwise. However, in these first few months of my life, as each domestic argument ended with a frustrated slap or a shake from Irene or from one of the many men who barged into the house as soon as Jack left for work, I must have sensed that I was not only a participant in but somehow one of the causes of all the noise and turmoil. Each hit, each shake, reinforced the curses and the threats that were more part of Jackie's and my regular diet than the food our mother could not afford to buy or neglected to prepare.

By the time Jackie was almost two years old, and I was eight months, she was already assuming a protective role, trying to shield me from the blows that would indiscriminately, unpredictably invade our play. When the Children's Aid Society "apprehended" us (yes, that's really the word they use), Irene's older sister having registered a complaint that we were being neglected and abused, my mother (according to a letter I received from my father in 1990) shrieked, "Take my babies, you goddamn fucking bitches. Take them both. I don't care. I can have as many babies as I want, but I'll tell you this. You'll never get another one away from me." Amid the turmoil Jackie was devastated at the thought of being separated from her little sister. She held onto me tightly, screaming (according to that same 1990 letter from Jack Fleming) "my baby, my baby." That was the last I saw of her, until we met, quite by chance and completely unaware that we were sisters, five years later.

A pretty child, with bright red curls and a generous smile to match her nature, Jackie was almost immediately adopted into a kindly middle-class family who lived in Transcona, a small railroading town, continental center of the Canadian National Railway, about ten miles east of Winnipeg.

With my constant whiny cry, emaciated body, and dark scowl, I was not so fortunate. Because of my cantankerous and uncooperative behavior, during the next few years—between the ages of eight months and three and a half years—I was moved from one foster home to another, eighteen moves in all. The Children's Aid Society had sterile, almost neutral-sounding euphemisms for the worst of these: "control homes" and "nonstimulative environments." A control home restrained its foster children through rigid rules and expectations. When rules were broken or expectations not met, the children were smacked or deprived of food. In nonstimulative homes, children were deprived of opportunities for play and interaction with each other or with the foster parents. There were few if any toys or books, and little interest was taken in the intellectual or social development of the foster children. As soon as CAS officials realized that they had placed one of their wards into a control home or nonstimulative environment, they tried to find more suitable foster parents, but until they succeeded the children were at the mercy of their caretakers.

I STILL SHUDDER AT THE MEMORY OF ONE OF THOSE FOSTER homes. This memory is provoked by but not specifically substantiated in what was read from my file, and can best be described as a memory of a recurring nightmare of a memory. I feel and smell as much as see the man, a huge, fat man with huge, fat hands. I hate those hands. They grab me when I come too close, and push themselves into my panties. His scratchy woolen shirt—I can still feel the roughness of those green and black squares when he would force me to sit on his lap—smells of beer and smoke, and when I try to squirm away, he laughs. Sharp slaps have taught me to sit very still and say nothing when he touches me. One time he grabs my hand and puts it on his bulging pants. I am so frightened that I urinate on him. I see myself tumbling down the basement stairs, wheels and handlebars rolling over me, screaming, then quiet, hearing him tell the story over and over again that I rode my tricycle down the basement stairs, knowing I didn't do that; knowing I am not so stupid that I would do that. White hospital sheets hold me tight to the bed, and still I have to hear him tell the nurses, the doctors, anyone who will listen, that I am so stupid I rode my tricycle down the basement stairs.

WHAT DID THE RECORD SAY ABOUT THAT—OR, AT LEAST THE portion of the record that was read to me? Not much. Just that I was hospitalized for several weeks after an incident at one of my foster homes. A few weeks prior to this, I had needed sutures on my eyelid, which I had, according to the record, tried to pry open with a can opener! As though it were an unrelated aside, the caseworker read a brief notation about my recurring fear of men.

Why was I, why were any children, placed into homes like this? These were war years, and a contingent of the Royal Canadian Air Force, stationed at Gimli, just an hour north of Winnipeg, was contributing substantially during furloughs in the city to the burgeoning illegitimate birth rate in Manitoba. There simply were not enough good homes to accommodate the number of children needing them. Those fortunate enough to be adopted at birth or soon after being taken over by the Children's Aid Society escaped the never-ending cycle of home after home after home. Those who were sickly or deformed or otherwise "unadoptable" entered a life often not much better than the one from which they had been wrenched. A portion of my Children's Aid Society record, in itself an intriguing literacy text of its time documenting what caseworkers consider to be key events in the life of a child, gives an idea of the life some of these children led.

SOCIAL HISTORY

Child: Karen Agnes Fleming, b. July 1, 1944.

Status: Temporary Ward: Children's Aid Society of Winnipeg

Family History:

Mother: Irene Fleming, b. March 22, 1925, of French origin. Mother failed out of school at grade six; had done domestic work and waitress prior to her marriage. Mother is described as an immature girl with hysterical tendencies, probably because of environmental conditions.

Father: Jack Fleming, b. 1923, of Dutch and German (Mennonite) origin. Separated from Irene when Karen was six months old.

Sibling: Jacqueline, b. August 5, 1943 [siblings born later were not added to the record]

March 25, 1945: Apprehended with Jackie. Malnourished, legs bowed with rickets, distraught, bad cough.

March 26, 1945: Taken to Mrs. Lenton. Screamed all night long.

March 27, 1945: Moved to Mrs. Munn. Happy there but pale and anemic.

April 4, 1945: Agency took control for six months. Still at Munns and by July weighed 21 pounds, 10 ounces.

August 24, 1945: Munns went on holiday, then moved. Karen reacting nervously at Munns.

August 25, 1945: Moved to Mrs. Peterson. Whooping cough. Frightened.

September 7, 1945: Moved to Mrs. Wilson. Nervous and frightened.

September 15, 1945: Moved back to Mrs. Munn. Walking alone. Taken off bottle; began toilet training. Physical spankings for spills and messes. Not well attended. No support. Began visits with mother and maternal grandfather but remained with Munns. Grandfather has alcohol problems. Neglect continued.

April 2, 1946: Testing authority; fear of doctors and men; toilet training an issue; bit new baby boy; difficult situation.

September 12, 1946: Moved to Mrs. Jones; lots of care and love.

November 17, 1946: New baby; need to move Karen again; she bit new baby.

January 15, 1947: Moved to Mrs. McLaughlin; lack of stimulation; Karen angry and frustrated.

February 4, 1947: Cut lid of eye with can opener; needed sutures; frightened. Fear of men noted.

March 17, 1947: Admitted to hospital; injured falling downstairs.

April 18, 1947: Moved to Mrs. Simmons; badly receding jaw; Dr. Brownlee gave her pearl button to suck to help jaw; increased fear of men.

The Simmonses were a British couple who wanted a little girl. According to the record, Mrs. Simmons and I got on splendidly, despite my developing tantrums and fears. She would hold me and hug me and smooth my hair and talk gently to me. Mr. Simmons tried to be very nice to me too, and never ever hurt me, but fear made an ice ball in my stomach whenever a man was in the same room and, according to the record, I would scream and run away and hide. One day, Mrs. Simmons gave me my very first doll. "You can call me Mommy," Mrs. Simmons told me, "and we'll call you Susie Simmons. Would you like that?"

Mommy? Susie Simmons? But I already had a mommy, so I had been told, even though I didn't remember anything about her. And even though my foster parents would call me whatever they wanted, I still knew that I had a name, and that name was mine. "I'm not Susie Simmons," I replied. "I'm Karen Agnes Fleming. And you can't be my mommy. I have a mommy, but my mommy ran away."

WHEN THE SOCIAL WORKER AT THE CAS READ ME THAT ACCOUNT in 1986, I felt awed by the sturdy sense of self in that not quite three-year-old girl who was both me and not me. Although I had no memory of that particular event, I could recall and the records confirmed that most of my foster homes had not been warm and caring, so I was curious about what had motivated such outright resistance in the face of unaccustomed kindness. My best guess, after seven years of mulling it over and talking with friends and colleagues, is that all I owned in the constant flux of homes and caretakers was my name. All the strangers I met, no matter what they ended up calling me, were told initially that I was Karen Agnes Fleming. The name was on my hospital charts and on every paper about me passed among the adults who sent me here and took me there. It was who I was, written down. At a very low level of consciousness, that insistence on sticking to my name as written down might be considered my first literate act, my first acknowledgment of the power of a name written down to designate a particular and constant version of reality.

The Simmonses were so taken aback by my intransigent reply that they reported the conversation to my caseworker, Mrs. Flynn, at the Children's Aid Society. A week later, they called Mrs. Flynn again, to tell her how they had overheard me playing with my doll. Its name? Susie Simmons.

They also reported how I played with Susie, how I would take off all her clothes and spank her and bite her, then tidy her up and pretend to have tea. They told of how I mutilated every doll and stuffed animal they gave me, by banging it against a wall and then discoloring one of its eyes. A photograph of me taken by the Simmonses, an enlarged and framed version of which now hangs in my adoptive mother's dining room, bears mute testimony to Mrs. Simmons' words. In it, I am seated at a little table with a child's tea set, determinedly shoving a graham wafer into a doll's mouth. The doll beside me, in frilly bonnet and dress, has her cheek and one eye smeared with what looks like nail polish. On a shelf behind me sits a little stuffed dog, its ear torn and its already black eye blackened even more. Beside it, just out of the camera's reach, a little stuffed kitten peers out from her own blackened eye.

The Simmonses persevered, but still I refused to allow Mr. Simmons anywhere near me. The Children's Aid Society was reluctant to begin the necessary procedures for me to be adopted into this situation, since I was still only a temporary ward, so when Mr. Simmons found employment in his British homeland, I once again began the cycle of moving from foster home to foster home.

I was furious at having been taken away from the friendliest place I had known. My behavior deteriorated from bad to downright destructive. I bit other children in the foster homes, I scratched myself as well as others, I screamed, and I swore. I began to dirty myself as well, seeming to find comfort in just sitting in my own messes. According to my record, "[Karen] was defiant, had a bad temper, wrecked toys and furniture, became self-destructive, would scratch and pinch herself and anyone near her, was 'a real bad apple.'" I was not yet three years old. Throughout this time, my fear and hatred of men continued to grow, so that I screamed or hid whenever a man entered the room.

So far, my recounting has been devoid of memory, except for the fat man with the fat hands, and dependent upon the records of the Children's Aid Society and letters written by my birth father. But now I am at the point of conscious memory or, to be more accurate, conscious memory fortified with the CAS records and letters from Jack Fleming. In December 1947, ten days before Christmas, my foster mother at the time gave me ten colored jelly beans to put under my pillow so that I could begin my count-down to Christmas and dream about it in color. I didn't really understand what Christmas was, but I knew it must be a very special time, because the house was filled with spicy, warm smells and pretty decorations. Counting out nine jelly beans the next night, eight the next, I sang the little jingle she taught me: "Goody, goody gumdrops, seven days till Christmas," "six days till Christmas," five days, four, three. And that's the end of the pleasant part, and the end of my introduction to Christmas. According to the record, two days before Christmas I was suddenly and unexpectedly removed from this home in preparation for spending the holiday with Irene, my mother.

ALL DAY LONG, I WAIT AT THE CHILDRENS AID SOCIETY RECEIVING Home while several other children are taken by family members or volunteers to spend Christmas Eve and Christmas at real homes. I sit all evening in one of the stuffed chairs in the parlor room, singing softly, "Goody, goody gumdrops, one more day till Christmas; goody, goody gumdrops, I'll see my mommy for Christmas." Knocks on the door. Hugs and presents all wrapped in pretty paper as one by one the children leave with strangers for Christmas. Will there be a present for me? I hope for Tinkertoys. In the hospital I played with Tinkertoys, and the nurses taught me how to build a bridge. Or, if not Tinkertoys, the shoe house with the old woman and all her children. Bright yellow, with ribbons that could be untied to let all the children go in and out. All the other kids are gone. Knock at the door. Is that for me? I hear a voice asking if Karen is still there. Someone's come for me. He brings in the cold, and shakes snow off his shoulder, and announces that my mother can't make it, that there is no place for me to go, that I will have to stay at the Receiving Home, and that the lady waiting for me to be taken so she can go home will have to stay with me. They are both angry. I have ruined their Christmas. I still have hope enough to ask, "Do you have a present?" He looks at me for the first time. I think for a moment that he is going to hit me, and get ready to bury myself in a cushion, but he reaches into his pocket and pulls out a grey chipped metal elephant, no bigger than my fist, and looks just as bad giving it to me as I feel taking it, ugly, cold grey thing.

YEARS LATER, I LEARNED FROM THE RECORDS AS WELL AS FROM Jack Fleming that Irene, trying to raise enough money to show her children—by this time she had given birth to another daughter, Susan—a good Christmas, had stolen the wallet of one of her "johns." Irene was spending that Christmas in jail. I spent it singing alone, in a prison of disappointment that I was finding increasingly difficult to escape.

Officially, I was not then up for adoption. Although taken from my mother and made a temporary ward of the court, I was still Irene's legal daughter, and Irene, having signed away her firstborn, was reluctant to sign away her second, especially since she had already given birth to Susan and was pregnant with a baby boy who would be called Michael. Apparently, she hoped one day to have all the family together. But the Fleming home, a firetrap boarding house in the central part of Winnipeg, was still no nurturing place for me. After a brief visit shortly following Irene's two-week lockup, I was found to be nervous, hungry, and dirty, and terrified of Irene's father, my grandfather, for reasons not specified.

Mrs. Flynn, my caseworker at the CAS, petitioned for me to be made a permanent ward of the Children's Aid Society, and a few attempts were made to find a suitable home for adoption despite Irene's reluctance to sign the forms. However, my bad temper, poor toilet habits, unappealing physical appearance, poor health—I suffered from rickets and had difficulty walking—ungracious manner, and terror of men made me an unlikely candidate. Unfortunately, the foster homes could no longer cope with my worsening disposition except by increasing my punishments, which only made my behavior more destructive. Needing the safety and stability of a "neutral environment" (a CAS euphemism for institutional care), I was moved permanently to the Receiving Home, which despite its brown-grey drabness I immediately named the Greenhouse.

If one can measure time in terms of fear, pain, and trauma, I lived at the Greenhouse for a very long time. Actually, I was there almost eight months, from just before I turned three until I was just past three and a half. None of the episodes that follow were entered in my official record—at least not in the parts that were read to me. How, then, can I remember them so vividly? I have two answers to that question. The first, which is just a hypothesis, is that when children grow up in a relatively stable environment, their memories of childhood become blended into a subconscious gestalt of undifferentiated images that supports their emotional and physical stability, and only those periodic episodes that threaten stability remain isolated in conscious memory. But when children grow up threatened in different ways from constantly changing sources, they become alert and wary. They take in and commit to conscious memory details they need for survival, psychological and emotional details no less important than material details such as a safe hiding spot. It might be a fleeting moment of happiness, such as the sparkle of sunshine on a river, to flood the mind with serenity when they need to wash away the pain of being hit. That's a mental trick I learned very early in life. It might be when to tell a lie, or when to be very still, in order to avoid being punished or abused. Because of the tremendous mental and emotional efforts required to cope with these events, they remain etched in memory.

In addition, I most likely remember these incidents because when I was between eight and twelve or thirteen, my adoptive mother would suggest on rainy days, when I had nothing to do, that I write about my life at the Greenhouse while I still was young enough to remember it. At the time, I did not view her suggestion as unusual. The typewriter was there, I was full of memories, and I was more than content to try to capture them in vocabulary and textual forms that I was learning at school. It was an irresistible invitation to become a more active participant in the world of literacy, which I had been appreciating ever since the Hamiltons had adopted me at age three and a half. I did not consider myself a good writer, a bad writer, or even a writer of any sort. It was something to do, an easy, risk-free entry into self-directed literacy. Only the typing itself was difficult, with no whiteout and limited amounts of paper. I typed slowly, with two fingers, to avoid making mistakes.

What I offer here as memories, then, is what I typed on my mother's ancient Underwood when I was eight to thirteen years old. I then would read to my mother what I had written, and she would ask questions whenever I seemed to depart from what she already knew or from what I had told her before. The re-creations in this book are a combination of my memory of these writings and readings, my mother's memory of these writings (she is ninety-two now), and some originals that have survived forty years among my mother's accumulation of books, notebooks, and papers.

Choosing what to write about was not difficult, but the actual writing immersed me in a cistern of sulfurous emotions that shaped the telling of remembered events. For example, when I initially wrote about the incident of being thrown down the stairs with my tricycle, I did not mention the probably catalytic event of urinating on that foster father in terror and angering him. I doubt that connection even occurred to me at age thirteen; rather, I was preoccupied by the recurring nightmare of stairs, tricycle, tumbling, and pain, and by the incongruity between his insistence that I had deliberately ridden my tricycle down the stairs and my conviction that I was not that stupid. And, at age thirteen, I was incapable of writing about his hands in my panties or his putting my hand on his groin, because by then I was old enough to understand shame and guilt, and that's what I felt. It was too unspeakable to write about.

I was not consciously trying to forge new connections and deeper understanding in these preadolescent writings, though I am certain that must have occurred. I was primarily trying to capture what happened in those earlier years and how I felt about it, and so wrote about only those bits of experience that were emotionally safe to recount. Not until after I encountered the official record and then met my siblings in 1986 did I begin to make the deeper connections that laced together and helped me understand the disparate events I recorded on those rainy day sessions at the typewriter.

This next memory was written in 1954, when I was nine years old. I was wearing a snuggly blue sweater on this particular rainy day, and it reminded me of another bright blue sweater six years earlier.

> I remember a sunny Sunday. Many of the children were being picked up by families who might want to adopt them. We were all dressed up in the best that the ladies who worked at the Greenhouse could find. I was wearing a yellow pleated skirt, a pretty white blouse with a lace-trimmed collar, and a bright blue, cozy sweater. Nobody owned any of the clothes, even when they had been given to us in foster homes. We just wore what the ladies put out for us, and I had never before been given such a wonderful outfit. I felt as pretty as the others. Nobody took me that day, but that was all right, because I was out in the sun, and once we were sure nobody was going to want me, I could go to the backyard and watch the brown, lazy river. I wanted to be closer. I didn't know it was against the rules to climb the fence, or maybe I did know and I just forgot, and I didn't know the wire would tear my skirt. Suddenly everyone was yelling at me and grabbing me away from the river, and I wasn't allowed out in the yard again for a long, long time.

Here's another account of my life at the Greenhouse, written when I was almost twelve and very concerned about my growing realization that I told lies as easily as I told the truth (but not sufficiently concerned yet to stop telling them when they suited my needs). And I was also becoming more consciously aware of the arbitrary power that adults have over children as well as of the need that people have for other people. This writing strikes me now, although I doubt it did then, as trying to work through some of these embryonic understandings.

I remember my first lie. At the Greenhouse, we weren't allowed back in the bedroom areas during the daytime unless we were sick. But for two or three days in a row, we heard howling from the area where the bigger boys' bedrooms were. Some of the older girls snuck upstairs to find out what was going on. They tried to keep me from coming, but I convinced them to let me tag along. We climbed the stairs slowly, trying to figure out the terrible sobs and muffled screams of "Don't make me" blotted out in an eerie silence, only to continue over again moments later. The biggest girl got closest, then flew down the stairs as quickly as she could, the rest of us scrambling after. The matron in the boys' room must have heard our scuffling, because she hollered out for everyone to stay put until she came downstairs. Then she slammed the door to the boys' room, and we couldn't hear so clearly anymore. Meanwhile, the girls were buzzing, "She was smashing his face down in his own shit. She just held his head and smashed it down until he couldn't breathe." At first I felt a strange kind of relief, because I only wet the bed most nights, and here was an older boy who was still dirtying his. But then he howled again, and I felt ashamed of my relief. He was in much worse trouble than ever I had been. We were horrified, and then grew terrified as we wondered what the matron would do to us. I began to cry, but some of the older girls tried to comfort me by saying that because I was the youngest, the matron probably wouldn't hurt me very much. "Tell her you didn't come upstairs," suggested one. "You can tell her we wouldn't let you."

"God kills those who lie," I said, with no idea of where I had heard that. I just knew that lies were very bad. The girls laughed and said that, with matron, it was better to lie. She marched down the stairs and lined us up, biggest to littlest. She was carrying a huge black hairbrush, which she waved with each question: "What were you doing upstairs? What did you see?" I was shaking, as each girl's knuckles received a good thwack from the hairbrush. Just before my turn came up, the girl in front of me said, "She didn't come with us. We thought she'd cry and get us in trouble, so we wouldn't let her come."

"Is that right, Karen?" and her steely eyes froze me. She knew, and I knew she knew, that I had been up there with the rest. But the older girl—I can't remember any of their names—had given me an out. All I had to do was take it, and if I didn't, she would be in even more trouble for lying on my behalf. I wondered why she had taken such a risk for me when she didn't even know me very well, and suddenly I felt a good feeling inside, a feeling that someone cared enough to put herself in danger. There really was no decision once I felt that warmth. "No" came out quite easily, "they wouldn't let me go upstairs." No hellfire, no sudden death, just the matron's "Well, you probably deserve a good smack anyway for all the things you've done that we haven't caught you at. Get along, then, where you're supposed to be."

I spent many hours of my growing up years trying to figure out the adults in charge of me, trying to determine how I could want so much to be good and yet always end up in trouble. This inability to escape trouble followed me wherever I went, from foster home to "protective" care to my adoptive home, and dominated my rainy day writing, as in the following two excerpts.

That matron was a scary one. Every night, after we had climbed into our beds, she would come into the room with a pillowcase over her head, clacking her false teeth at the end of her tongue. "I'll get you if you get out of bed, and if I get you, I'll eat you, so stay in bed until morning," she would screech at us. I would lie in bed, making myself as flat and as still as possible, not daring to move the sheets even a wrinkle for fear she would swoop down at me, needing to go to the bathroom but terrified that she would catch me. I don't think I ever thought she would really eat me, but I was pretty sure she would give me a good hit. I wet the bed almost every night.

I remember one time I was good for a whole week. That was really special, because no matter how hard I tried, and I think I really did try—I didn't want to be bad, mostly because I didn't want to be hit—I would spill, or fall and dirty my clothes, or swear, or lose my temper and hit or bite someone, or wet myself. But one whole week went by without any bad things. The ladies were so excited that they decided I could be taken to the corner store, a little over a block away, for a treat. This was wonderful. I hadn't been allowed out much since I had almost fallen into the river, and I hadn't left the Greenhouse for a long, long time. They dressed me up nicely, though I can't remember anymore what I wore, and I set off, firmly in the grip of one of the ladies. Not the nicest one, not the one I liked best, who would sing when she changed the bed and not yell at me when she found it wet, but at least it was not the awful matron.

We went into the store and sat at the fountain. When the clerk asked me what I wanted, I didn't know how to answer him, because I don't think anybody had ever asked me that before. "What do I want?" I repeated stupidly. The lady answered for me, "A Coca-Cola for each of us." It came in one of those curved glasses, wide at the brim and narrowing down, and the brown liquid fizzled and tickled my nose. I lifted the cool glass up to let the fizzes prickle the tip of my nose, and then it happened. I must have breathed in at the wrong time, because up my nose went the Coke, and I choked, and dropped the glass and the Coke all over the floor. I just looked at it, waiting for the words I knew would come. And they did, in a torrent. "You just can't be good, can you. You can't even be taken to the corner store without causing a mess." She said a whole lot more, but I don't even want to write it down.

One day in the winter of 1947—a day that I don't remember but reconstruct here from the records and from the memories of Katherine and William Hamilton, my adoptive parents—I was in the Greenhouse playroom in my customary place in the corner, banging a nondescript piece of block against the floor. The rest of the children were playing some kind of game with the playroom leader. The door opened, and the Hamiltons entered the room. The Hamiltons were not the typical couple looking for a child to adopt. In the first place, they already had a child of their own, Bill, Jr., at that time almost eight years old. In the second place, they were older than most adoptive parents. Having married relatively late in life, at thirty-seven—first marriages for both of them—they were now in their mid-forties. And third, unlike most adoptive parents, they were not looking for a newborn but preferred an older child. They lived on a small farm on the outskirts of Winnipeg, with Bill's mother, in her seventies, and a foster child, Joe, in his late teens.

Joe was not a Children's Aid Society foster child but rather the son of a foreman who had worked for Bill, a general contractor, in Baltimore. Just as the Hamiltons had been about to leave the United States in apprehension of the war fever that followed the bombing of Pearl Harbor, eleven-year-old Joe had arrived on their doorstep. His parents had been killed in an auto accident, and he was terrified that he was going to be placed in an orphanage. "Take me with you, please," he had begged. Bill Hamilton, aware of the red tape involved in an official adoption, and of the impossibility of a foster child arrangement for an American citizen in a new country, hesitated. Katherine, on the other hand, saw no regulations, only a skinny, scared boy who was reaching out for her assistance. Joe was stuffed among the household goods in the back seat of the car, and they left together to begin a new life in Canada.

While Bill was establishing himself as a general contractor in Winnipeg, Katherine became accustomed to looking after her son, her mother-in-law, and her now legally documented foster child while tending a flock of chickens on the tiny farm. Not knowing how to drive, and with the nearest regular bus stop over two miles away, she was stuck on the farm from dawn until dark, unable to leave Billy with her mother-in-law for a moment. The elder Mrs. Hamilton's memory was going. Billy had almost drowned one day when she was giving him a bath and had badly burned himself on the stove another time while she was looking after him in the kitchen. Joe was still in school, although that would not last much longer, as neither Joe nor the school was getting anything much out of the other. Reading in the paper one day about the overcrowded conditions at the Children's Aid Society Receiving Home, and about the children who needed places to live, Katherine decided that she had time and space to spare and that she should share it with someone less fortunate. A little girl might be nice company. Since the bulk of the responsibility for the child would be hers, she easily convinced Bill to consider the idea.

The Hamiltons entered the playroom at the Greenhouse and watched the children involved in their games. Bill moved from child to child, talking gently with each little girl. Katherine listened and watched as the relative merits of each little girl were laid out for her. Turning, she noticed me, alone and in the corner. "What about that one. You haven't told me anything about her."

My mother was amazed at the matron's response, which she can still recall almost word for word. "Oh. That's Karen, but you wouldn't be interested in her. I doubt that you'd be able to have her even if you wanted her. She has a lot of problems. She has a temper you wouldn't believe in one so young, and a long list of swear words to match. She can't get along with anyone, child or adult. Just sits and plays her own little games all by herself. She's had some bad experiences in her foster homes, and the doctor thinks that she may never be able to leave the care of the Children's Aid. She doesn't walk very well, because her legs are bowed from rickets, and she's had whooping cough and diphtheria both in the last six months, so she's kind of sickly. She's uncooperative, and still wets herself and her bed. She doesn't seem to be able to learn anything she's told. She can't abide men. She yells and kicks and runs whenever a man goes near her. The doctor figures she'll probably not finish school or ever be able to hold a job. Not one for you to consider."

"But she's just a little girl. She can't be that bad."

"Well, as I said, she's had some bad experiences, and they've decided that if she has another bad experience in a foster home, that'll be the end of her, if you know what I mean." She rolled her eyes as she mouthed the word *Brandon* in reference to the provincial home for severely retarded and emotionally handicapped children. Bill Hamilton began to move toward me "the same way I'd approach a scared little puppy," he told me many years later. He moved slowly, making just enough noise so that he wouldn't startle me. I knew he was near and my banging got quicker and louder. He stopped and waited. I banged and banged, then stopped and looked. Our eyes met and held, while Bill slowly reached inside his coat pocket for a piece of licorice allsorts. Again very slowly, he reached toward me, but not near enough to touch me. To get the candy, I would have to reach out toward him. Neither moved. The matron and Katherine watched. My eyes moved from Bill's face to the candy, then back to Bill's face, then back to the candy. I reached out and took it, popped it into my mouth, then picked up the block, ready to recommence banging. "No," said Bill, very calmly. "Put that down and come here." He knelt down slowly and stayed very still. I came toward him and stopped within inches. "What's your name?" he asked.

"Karen," I replied. "What's yours?"

The matron stood amazed. Katherine, more accustomed to Bill's way with children and animals, and less familiar with my history, was less surprised. She faced the matron. "Anybody will take these pretty, happy, healthy children. I've got time on my hands and lots of room for her to stretch out those weak legs. I'll take her."

2

Orphans Belong in Orphanages

Behind the visible words of every written text there lurks the writer's context, his or her life in the world and in the mind, in actions and in language. The words of the text are laden with the meanings of their time and place, augmented by the writer's reading as well as by the assumptions of the culture. To the reading of any text, the reader similarly brings her or his context and his or her language with different assumptions and other reading experiences. The conflux of reader and writer seems to make the giving and receiving of a simple, incontrovertible message impossible.

—M. Meek, *On Being Literate*, 35

One reader of an early draft of this chapter told me that she could not understand why a child would fear going through a door held by an adult. In her world, adults do not strike or kick kids going through doors. In my early world, they did. What was unthinkable to her, and therefore resistant to understanding in the text, was a given to me. Not only did her comment prompt me to be more explicit, it highlighted a significant function of literacy and of the literacy narrative. Since we cannot—and would not want to—live all possible lives, literacy enables us, however imperfectly, to begin to enter the life of another. It enables us to make a start at understanding and then possibly helping those whose worlds have not enabled them sufficiently to help themselves.

"YOU CAN'T BE SERIOUS. BRINGING A CHILD OF THE STREETS into your home! That's foolish. That's ridiculous! How are you going to find time to look after Mother? How are you going to find time to look after your own son? You don't know anything about her. She could grow up and poison you or kill you all in your beds. You read about that sort of thing happening all the time. Orphans belong in orphanages. That's what we have them for. You don't know what you're doing!"

It was my first weekend visit with the Hamiltons. Behind a closed door, just off the living room where I was building a house with yellow and red blocks, Bill's two sisters, visiting from Baltimore, were sharing their thoughts with Katherine. "We're not going to allow Mother to stay here, that's for certain. That child swears a blue streak. How do you think she picked that up? And that song she's always singing, 'Give me wine, whiskey, and wild, wild women.' What kind of song is that for a three-year-old girl to sing? Imagine what her background has been. Imagine what she could grow up to be. A streetwalker, probably, just like her mother. She'll be pregnant before she's fifteen. She'll be nothing but trouble. You'll see. Change your mind, and we'll leave Mother here. But if you insist on having this, this . . ."

By this time, I realized that once again not only were the adults who had come into my life yelling at each other but also I was the cause of the yelling. I didn't know what a streetwalker was, or what pregnant was, but I knew they must be bad, because here was just like everywhere else. No matter where I was, I was bad. I tore apart the wall of the house I had been trying to build, grabbed the blocks by the fistful, and hurled them at the wall of the living room as hard as I could, yelling, "Bad blocks. You stupid, ugly, goddamn bad blocks. You can't make a stupid house. You can't even make a stupid goddamn wall."

And then the black came, as it so often had before, as though my eyes somehow turned inward to my soul and saw only darkness and badness. The black would wash over me so that I lost all awareness of anything outside of me, and I would scream and bang my head against the wall or floor and pound my heels as hard as I could, screaming, kicking, and pounding until I exhausted myself. I had only brief warning of the black coming, like a tidal wave seen seconds before it hits, and I knew that after I would be punished, but I had not yet found a way to stop the force of it.

With a satisfied told-you-so huff, my potential aunts opened the door, letting Katherine through to deal with me.

My second weekend visit went considerably better. Arriving for dinner on a Friday evening two weeks after my first visit, I noticed that the older, cranky lady was not there. Nor were the two other ladies who had done all the yelling. There were just Katherine and Bill and Billy and Joe. As we sat around the dinner table, I heaped my plate high with fluffy, creamy mashed potatoes, ladled them richly with gravy, then surrounded them with a huge helping of everything on the table before I started to eat, a survival technique I had learned at the Greenhouse, where, if I didn't take all the food I wanted as quickly as I could the first time around, I wasn't likely to have a chance at any more.

Watching with an amused twinkle while I filled my plate as full as I could get it, Bill spoke, "You can have anything you want to eat, and as much of it as you want, but remember this: you need to eat everything that you put on your plate."

"Oh, don't worry," I replied with gusto, "I will." And I did, amid the amazed looks of the Hamiltons, who had never seen anyone except six-foot teenage Joe eat so heartily and enjoy it so much.

The food is what I remember most about that second visit. I woke the next morning to one of the most tantalizing aromas I had ever smelled. I followed my nose downstairs to the kitchen to find golden pieces of something on the plates already set at the table. "What's that wonderful stuff?"

"Toast. It's only toast," was Katherine's reply.

"Toast! Toast isn't like that. Toast is cold and dark and doesn't have that soft runny stuff on it."

"That soft runny stuff is butter, and that's the way we make toast here."

"Mmmmmmmm," stuffing my mouth with a huge bite, "I love it."

My third visit was to be the deciding one, for both the Hamiltons and me. It was a whole week long, and it started on St. Valentine's Day. I remember that because when the Hamiltons came to get me, Katherine hugged me and called me her "precious little valentine." It was the nicest thing anyone had ever said to me; it was also the only time I can recall her using a direct term of endearment with me. Wanting to make the stay special for me, and wanting to make me feel at home, Billy decided at bedtime to offer me one of his most treasured possessions. He dashed upstairs, grabbed something from his room, then yelled proudly from the top of the stairs,

"Guess what I have for you behind my back?" The only thing I had ever received following this behind-the-back ritual was candy, so the last thing I expected was Billy racing down the stairs at full tilt and shoving a brown furry thing within an inch of my face. I was terrified. I had never seen anything like this and screamed and hid behind the huge living room chair. Crouched as tiny as I could make myself, I shivered and sobbed. Billy was flabbergasted. His gesture had been sincerely intended, and he had no idea how to respond to this outburst of rejection. "Look, it's only a teddy bear. It's just a little brown teddy bear. It won't hurt you."

"Bears bite," I sniffled, still crouched in a tremble.

"This is a toy bear. It can't bite. It's not real; it's not alive. It can't hurt you. You're supposed to sleep with it."

I didn't know what he was talking about. "Sleep with a bear? Sleep with that thing in my bed? I can't sleep with that. It'll bite me in the middle of the night." And I crouched smaller, quivering and cold with my fear. Yet a part of me was beginning to see how ridiculous my position was, since the bear was obviously not biting Billy, and I was trying to figure how to get out of it.

But I was too late. "Look, I'll show you it can't hurt you," said Billy, so upset by my fright that he felt some drastic action was in order. He grabbed the little teddy's head and twisted its neck so violently that its head finally came off. It was not a quick process, and by the time he was finished, I was a shaking mess of fear that my head might be next. Katherine was furious that Billy had wrecked his teddy bear, a gift from his Aunt Bella, Katherine's older sister, and dumbfounded by my excessive reaction. With her best stern-Presbyterian demeanor, she calmed us and sent us to our beds.

That teddy bear story has remained with me as a symbol of personal marginalization within a literary heritage. Teddy bear stories abound in children's literature and in adults' written memories of their childhood, and every one that I have read or heard connects the teddy bear with love and security or with some loss within a framework of love and security. My teddy bear story, though now it seems pretty innocuous, helps me to understand the irrational fears of a little girl who had never slept with a cuddly toy, who could not understand giving or receiving, and who was terrified and confused by the sudden violence in a little boy who had tried to be generous.

That was the start of my fear of Billy that for many years underlay all my other emotions about him. Not until I began to write this story did I think of how difficult it must have been for him, an only child for eight years, the pride of his parents, loved and cosseted by them, to be suddenly confronted by this wimpy waif who would steal some of their attention from him. I felt fear and envy, and some moments of camaraderie while we were growing up, but not, until recently, sympathy. And this sympathy was born of some better understanding, engendered by writing this narrative, of the challenges he had been forced to face.

When Mrs. Flynn came to pick me up, her question hung in the air, strangely unanswerable. "Well, Karen, would you like to stay here for good?" We were all in the kitchen, and I was coated up ready to leave. I looked around and thought of the wonderful food, of the stories Katherine had read to me while I snuggled beside her on the soft sofa. I thought of the candies that Bill would pretend to hide so that I could easily find them and of how Billy had shown me how to play with the sticky blocks and had run his electric train round and round in its tracks for me to watch. "If I say yes can I just stay? Right now, for ever and ever?"

"No," said Mrs. Flynn. "You have to come back with me for a few days while we work everything out."

A few days seemed unimaginable. "No. I don't want to come back here. I just want to go someplace and stay. I hate always coming and going. If you take me back to the Greenhouse, I'm going to stay there." Then I ran toward Katherine and flung my arms around her hips. "Don't let them take me away," I begged. "Don't make me go away." At the same time, I remember a strangely paradoxical state of mind: afraid of the matron at the Greenhouse, scared that I wouldn't see Sally anymore, the nice woman who chose pretty clothes for me to wear, scared that the matron would hit me if she thought I was going to leave, yet confused about why she would want me to stay when she hated me. All those fears swarmed over me, adding up to an illogical dilemma: should I be loyal to those who had been feeding and clothing me for several months now, or should I be loyal to these new people who offered a new yet strange environment? And now I wonder why they were even pretending that the decision was in any way mine.

Mrs. Flynn took charge, disengaged me from Katherine, and promised to try to arrange everything as quickly as possible.

I still remember the day I finally left the Greenhouse. I was so excited that I must have run up and down the stairs dozens of times, not caring a bit about the rules. Sally was packing my suitcase, and I wanted to make sure that she put in my favorite dress, all striped with bright colors. I had worn it only once, but I loved that dress. I couldn't see it anywhere and was terribly worried that she wouldn't pack it, even though she kept saying that she'd try to find it.

Then the Hamiltons arrived. Mrs. Hamilton, now to be Mom, was wearing a lilac crepe dress under a black Persian lamb coat and carrying the coziest looking matching muff. Mr. Hamilton, now Dad, had a warm, comfortable looking topcoat and a jaunty hat. And, as I was already getting used to, a licorice allsort for me. Looking at their splendid clothes and friendly faces, I thought that maybe from now on I would be safe. I wouldn't have to worry anymore about matron or about being hit. Bundled up in an ugly black coat far too big for me, I felt unworthy of their splendor, but then I thought of the marvelous striped dress in my suitcase that I would show them as soon as we got "home" and figured that I had something that would make them feel proud that they had me now.

It was a spring day in early March. The sun was disintegrating the remnants of old snow as I eagerly looked out the car window for the increasingly familiar landmarks on the five-mile journey from the Greenhouse to the farm. As soon as we arrived, Mom and Dad told me to go outside and enjoy the sunshine while they unpacked my small brown suitcase. I could go anywhere I wanted, except down to the Seine, the narrow muddy river that separated our farm from the one next to it, since the ice was too thin.

Wanting to be good, I asked Billy which way to the river, so I would be sure not to go that way. Somehow, even though I went in the opposite direction from his pointing finger, I ended up walking through the wood fringe that led down to the banks. Sure enough, there were blackly spreading holes breaking through the ice cover. I felt a lump of fear and guilt growing in my chest, making me breathe faster and faster as I realized I was in the one place I had been told not to go. I stood there paralyzed, hoping nobody would catch me right where I wasn't supposed to be, when all of a sudden I was in the water. I don't remember how I got there, or even how cold it must have felt. I didn't even have time to yell before Billy was there to pull me out and drag me back to the house.

Scolded and then plunged into a hot bath, I suffered my final humiliation when I discovered that not only had the beautiful striped dress not been put into the suitcase but even my comfortable flannel nightgown from the Greenhouse had not been packed. Instead, new blue-and-white-striped, stiff cotton pajamas were waiting for me on my bed. Remembering a picture of prisoners' striped clothes in one of Billy's comic books, I was terrified I was going to be sent to jail for disobeying and refused to put them on. Shivering cold, not caring one bit that I was being thoroughly bad, I stood naked, refusing to put on those ugly pajamas. Mom said, "Fine. But don't come downstairs until you do." With that, she closed the door to my new bedroom and left to get supper ready.

"Jailbird," I muttered to myself between clenched teeth, a term that I had learned from that same comic book that had prejudiced me against striped pajamas. "Here I am just a goddamn jailbird my first night here.

They'll never keep me now. I'm bad and I'm ugly, and I'm so stupid. How could I go into the water? I knew I wasn't supposed to go there, and I ended up in it anyway. It's not fair."

"What's not fair?" said Dad, who had come upstairs to see what the fuss was all about. "Get your pajamas on so I can come in and talk to you." He didn't hit me. He didn't yell at me. He just gently sat down beside me, looked me straight in the eye, and asked me again, "What's not fair?"

"I look like a stupid jailbird. I want you to like me. I want to be good and to look pretty so you will like me, and I just can't do it. I didn't want to get wet. I didn't even want to go near the river. I just ended up there." I went on and on, while he listened. When I finally exhausted all my anxieties, he put his hands on my shoulders, looked me in the eyes again, and told me words I can never forget because they weren't anything that I wanted to hear: "Don't ever bother about life being fair. Life is never fair. Just do what you're told, and don't tell lies. You can be as good as anybody else. All you have to do is try. Now, you can come down and join the family for supper, or you can stay in this room and go to bed. But if you come downstairs, I want no more crying or sulking about. If you're going to live here, you have to do what you're told, and do it with a smile on your face."

I was stunned. I had hoped he would put his arms around me. I had hoped he would tell me everything would be all right. I had hoped impossibly. But there was one important lesson I learned from that talk: I could be good, if only I could figure out how. But the responsibility would be all mine, and it wasn't going to be easy.

I came downstairs, still feeling like a jailbird in my striped pajamas. Not even the smell of supper cheered me up, but I didn't dare look sad after Dad's admonition, so I lifted up the muscles in my eyebrows and the edges of my mouth in what I hoped was a satisfactorily cheerful look.

"We've been talking," said Dad, as I took my place at the table. "We've decided that you need a complete break with the Greenhouse and with all that went on there. We want you to forget Karen. There is no more Karen. You're going to have a new name to match your new life. From now on, we're going to call you Sharon. I never liked the name Karen anyway: it makes me think of carrion."

"What's carrion?" I asked.

"Dead meat," he replied. Billy snorted into his glass of milk, and I felt robbed and excited at the same time. I didn't have my colorful striped dress, I didn't have my warm, comfortable nightgown, and I didn't even have my name. They were all wrong and bad. From now on, I would be Sharon. And I could be good, because Karen, who was always bad, wouldn't be around anymore.

"You don't need to come inside. There's nothing dangerous outside. It's only a dog," she said. "You'd better get used to it, because he lives in the barn with a couple of others, and they have the run of the place. They don't bite or snap so long as you don't provoke them."

Beginning to realize that outside held even more hazards and challenges than inside, I tried to figure out a strategy. Dogs lived here. I lived here. We obviously had to find some way to get along together. For now, counting to ten would not do. The dog came nearer, pinning me against the door, looking up at me, his tongue lolling and drooling, just like the wolf I had seen in the book *Little Red Riding Hood* that Mom had read to me my last weekend here. But surely she wouldn't have left me outside with a creature who would eat me for dinner. I reached toward him, and he jerked his head up. I jerked back. I guess he thought it was a game because then he jumped on me. Startled, I fell onto his back. He growled and snapped at me so I lost my balance and tumbled against the concrete basement wall, scraping a bloody gash on my head. Seeing the blood, I screamed, but that didn't bring me any help. Once I realized that I wasn't really hurt, I stood up. The dog was watching me warily [Hey, I got *warily* in, Mom. That was the last one on the list], and I was watching him just as warily. Suddenly, I thought I understood. He wanted to be friends. He just didn't like my falling on top of him. But how could I safely test this new understanding? I sat on the back step, holding my head, the blood from my gash seeping through my fingers. The dog came up and licked it off. "Ah, that's what dogs do. They lick." So I licked him back, and we sat there licking each other until Mom looked out the window and put a stop to that. But we had made friends, and I had one less worry the next time I went outside.

Those early days at the Hamiltons, full of unprecedented events, remain etched in memory. Soon after my arrival, Mom returned home from shopping with a bundle especially for me. "You mean they're all mine?" I could hardly believe it. Three pairs of soft, warm cotton stockings, three vests as white as white could be, six pairs of underpants, pink and blue and white, a pair of snugly, warm flannelette pajamas to make up for the stiff, starched cotton ones, a yellow dress with pink and blue flowers embroidered on the smocked bodice, a white pinafore to protect the dress, two pairs of corduroy overalls, one red and one blue, three striped shirts to wear with them, and a pair of shiny brown shoes. I had never seen so many things for me all at one time in one place, and all brand new. After trying on every single item, I folded them carefully away in my drawer at the bottom of a dresser. About fifteen minutes later, I took them all out again and laid them on my bed, stroking their soft, clean newness, singing to myself, "They're all mine, and they're all brand new."

Later that day, when Mrs. Ackroyd from across the street came to visit Mom, I pulled her upstairs to see my display of finery, proudly pointing out that "they're all mine, and they're all brand new." Of course, Dad was also forced to see them when he came home, as was his friend, Mike Keweriga, when he came over to talk about the spring planting. Only when I tried to lure the hapless newspaper delivery boy up the stairs and into my room to view my bonanza did Mom put a stop to it. Even so, for the next week, every morning after I made my bed, I took everything out that I was not already wearing and laid it lovingly, piece by spotless piece, on the bed, truly amazed at the beauty of new, clean clothes.

And I was so happy that I wanted to hug everyone I met, especially— to my own and everyone else's amazement—men. My fear of men suddenly and completely reversed itself, so that I threw my arms around every man who came to the house. It was a startling turnaround, and Mom was advised by the Children's Aid Society caseworker, who regularly checked on my progress with the Hamiltons, to explain to me that such behavior was not appropriate. I then focused all my admiration and devotion onto my father, following him around everywhere and even waiting forlornly outside the bathroom door whenever he was inside. I was devastated when, within a few short weeks of my coming to the Hamiltons, he left with no explanation—at least to me—for over a month.

That spring was a rich time of discovery as I was terrified by the screeching of a nestful of newly hatched robins that fell from one of the huge oak trees, enchanted by the wriggly little worms that wound around my fingers on warm sunny days at the manure pile, and most concerned at the way the mother cats in the barn toted their babies around, jaws securely holding them by the scruffs of their necks. I had no idea that the smell of manure was offensive to others, that worms were not playthings, that birds were not threatening, and that kittens were customarily carried that way. But day by day, as the warm sun brought more and more of the farm to life, I learned. Outdoors, I learned by myself. Indoors, my world was expanding even more.

Every morning, after the breakfast dishes were done, I picked one of the big orange books from the twelve-volume *Childcraft Encyclopedia* that the Hamiltons had bought soon after Billy was born, and Mom read to me. This was my favorite time of the day, the only time that was just ours. We sat side by side on the huge overstuffed chesterfield. Mom held the chosen book while I snuggled into the brown velvet bolster, a plump, sausage-

NOW AT AGE FIFTY, AS I RECALL THAT FIRST DAY AS A HAMILTON, I am angry. I had stood up for Karen when the Simmonses wanted to call me Susie and yet, not even a year later, I gave up my name without even a small regret. I'm unsure whether I am angry at myself for not resisting, or angry at my new family for trying to eliminate my previous identity, or angry because they connected me with dead meat. I was not angry at the time, because they rarely called me by my name anyway. Dad and Bill half the time called me Floozie and half the time Susie—I seemed destined to be called Susie one way or another—except when I was very dirty. Then Dad would call me Gravel Gertie, and Mom would call me the Wreck of the Hesperus. These nicknames seemed friendly enough, and I welcomed them. Still, in retrospect, I admire the almost-three-year-old Karen for resisting Susie Simmons more than the almost-four-year-old Sharon for accepting Sharon, Susie, Floozie, and Gravel Gertie. Karen had more sense of self. Sharon was too early learning to compromise pragmatically for survival.

"MOM," THE TWELVE-YEAR-OLD ME CALLS FROM THE DINING room table, where the typewriter sits, to the kitchen, where my mother, recovering from a two-week bout with sciatica and therefore home from her job as a resource teacher at a school in nearby Transcona, is baking an apple pie. "Can I write about the old striped dress and the new striped dress in the same memory, even though they're seven years apart? Because I think it's so wonderful that you remembered how miserable I was that first day, even though you never said anything at the time, and I think it's so wonderful that you went out and bought that beautiful dress with the multicolored striped skirt yesterday because you still remembered. How can I get all that in the same memory? And I also want to get in how Dad always laughs whenever Billy says, 'Stupidest thing I ever did was to pull Susie out of the river that day.' Can I mix the past and the present in one memory?"

"You can write whatever you like. Just figure it out and write it. And don't shout from one room to another."

"I'm trying to use some of the words we learned in our vocabulary lessons this week. I've got *admonition* and *disintegrate* and *plunge* and *prejudiced* and *profound* so far. How's that?"

"Good. Remember what I always tell you: 'Use a new word ten times and it's yours.'"

And so I write whenever the weather keeps me inside and I have nothing new to read. At the same time, I become fascinated with learning, especially with how children learn about the world that surrounds them, partly because I am old enough at twelve to realize that what I had learned between ages three and four were features of life that most children had learned much earlier, and partly because my mother has been tutoring a boy five years older than me, born with muscular dystrophy, and I have seen and heard him move from a nonliterate to a literate state. Bobby Peron, the son of my father's foreman, comes weekly to our home on his special tricycle when weather permits and, having no access to public schooling, learns from my mother to read and to work with numbers. It is a miracle of learning happening before my eyes and ears, and it fascinates me.

I also begin consciously to incorporate not only the vocabulary we are learning at school but also the figures of speech—especially similes, metaphors, alliteration, and personification—that intrigue me during our study of poetry. Much of their attraction comes from their immediate source, my eighth-grade English teacher, on whom I have an adolescent crush that motivates me not only to memorize every single poem we are studying and half of Shakespeare's *A Midsummer Night's Dream* but also to be drawn toward the profession of teaching English.

What follows is a re-creation of one of those writings in which I tried to work vocabulary words from our *Words Are Important* text into an assignment that asked us to recall a time from our early childhood when we learned something new.

I remember the first time I saw a dog. It seems strange to be almost four years old and not know what a dog was. Mom believed that the best things for a growing girl are sunshine and fresh air, so right after breakfast on my second day at the farm, after being admonished [I got another one in, Mom, *admonish*] to absolutely never go near the river, I found myself again on the doorstep, ready to walk into my new world. A path wove itself through the remains of the snow, darkly different from the patches of grass sweeping down to the road on one side and over to the chicken coop and garden on the other. I started down the path, thinking I might explore around the barn, when a strange creature hurtled toward me. I slammed myself against the door, closed my eyes, and counted to ten. In the past, that had sometimes worked when the matron was on a rampage [I got *rampage* in, too, Mom]. Often, by the time I reached ten, she'd have moved on to bully someone else. I peeked to see that creature still sniffing around the yard. I closed my eyes and counted to ten again but with no better luck. I banged on the door. "Mom, let me in. There's a horrible thing out here, and he's going to bite me."

shaped cushion. Together we entered an imaginary world of fairies, elves, and princesses, angry kings and marauding pirates, talking animals with good and bad habits just like people, all spurred on by impossible ambitions that somehow were able to be realized, although always at some cost. I soon had four favorites that I chose in order on a four-day cycle: *Nursery Rhymes and Poems*, *Longer Nursery Rhymes and Poems*, *Myths and Legends*, and *Folk and Fairy Tales*. There was one fairy tale that I especially liked, about a princess who lived happily ever after even though she didn't marry her prince, because the princess was sometimes naughty, just as I was, and because the princess had brown hair, which I had, when most princesses were pictured with yellow hair. I also loved the poem about "the land where the Jumblies live;/ Their heads are green, and their hands are blue,/ And they went to sea in a sieve."

"How could they sail in a sieve?" I asked every time, envisioning the water running through the holes and drowning everyone. And Mom replied, "In books, anything can happen."

Anything can happen. In books, anything can happen. Why not in real life? It was the first connection I recall making between literature and life. And it became almost like a mantra, "anything can happen, anything can happen," helping me cope with the times that were not so good. And there were many of those.

LIVING ON A FARM MEANT HAVING FEW NEIGHBORS AND EVEN FEWER children my own age to play with. But across the road lived a boy just a year older than me, Jimmy Ackroyd, with flaming red hair and an exuberant sense of adventure. While our older siblings were at school, Jimmy showed me how to run alongside my brother's Shetland pony, Tiny, without frightening him or getting in the way of his hooves. He showed me where the Seine narrowed into a shallow stream that in dry periods could be crossed, and he showed me trees to climb. One day we were sitting on the banks of the Seine, talking and sucking on cylinders of straw from the loft in the barn, when he asked me, "What's *adopted*?"

Knowing nothing about natural children or childbirth, I didn't have the easy answer I could have given a few years later. "It's when you don't really belong in a family," I replied, thinking of the baby pictures of Billy in almost every room of the house, and of the stories of Queenie, the family dog that had died just before I came, and of the whole fabric of shared history that I was not a part of. And my ears filled with memory of the constant reminder whenever I was naughty, which was just about every day. "It's when you have to be grateful for having clothes on your back, a roof over your head, and food in your stomach. If you're not adopted, you just have all that automatically." And suddenly—it might have been the first stirring of this emotion, certainly the first that I remember—I felt a burst of resentment at having to meet a different set of standards, rules, and expectations than other children, particularly my new brother, who didn't seem to be expected to be grateful for anything. "Do you have to be grateful for having clothes on your back, a roof over your head, and food in your stomach?" I asked Jimmy. Something in my tone alerted Jimmy to my change of mood, and he responded with uncustomary insensitivity, "Of course not, dummy. I guess that's just for orphans."

The black started to come. I tried to fight it back, because I really liked Jimmy and didn't want to risk his friendship. At my upraised arm, Jimmy jumped up and ran. In fierce and furious chase we bolted pell-mell up from the banks of the peaceful Seine, through low brush and woods, toward Tiny's pasture. The running somehow dissipated my black mood, and I called out, "Hey Jimmy, it's okay. I'm not mad anymore." Jimmy turned around, still running. I yelled, "Watch out!" and he turned again, smack into the barbed wire fence enclosing the pasture. He collapsed from the impact, as the barbs tore his face, arms, and legs. Terrified, I ran home, screaming, "I've killed Jimmy! I've killed Jimmy!"

The adults sorted it all out, in the process finding a rusty butcher knife nearby that I had never touched, had never before seen. The story rearranged itself among the adults so that with murderous intent I chased Jimmy through the woods brandishing a butcher knife. I was hauled away from the scene of the crime in shame, and Jimmy was forbidden to play with me. That night came the first of many explicit threats to return me to the Greenhouse. The next day Jimmy broke out in chicken pox, which may have accounted for his deep faint on impact with the fence the previous day, and which also may have prevented him from telling what really happened. At the time, however, I didn't know that. All I knew was that everyone thought I had tried to kill Jimmy, and for some reason Jimmy did not deny it. I began to wonder whether I really might be as bad as everyone thought. Branded a liar and a potential murderer by my new neighbors, with similar doubts and apprehensions creeping into the minds of my new parents and even trickling into my own growing sense of self, I buried myself in my bed wishing that I would never have to leave it.

And I didn't, for almost two weeks. When I slept, I dreamt about that rusty butcher knife, the rust distorted by my bewilderment into Jimmy's blood, and I woke up wondering if I really had tried to kill Jimmy, worrying that I must be some kind of horrible monster. About ten days after the incident, while I was in my darkened bedroom still recovering from my own bout of chicken pox complicated by measles, with a darkened mind confused by guilt and fear of being returned to the Greenhouse, Mrs. Ackroyd and Jimmy came to the house to leave me a present, a girl's mirror and comb set. They couldn't come in to see me because of the quarantine, but I knew that finally the story had been set straight and that I wouldn't have to endure the misgivings and distrust any longer. At least in relation to that event.

But my brother, the same age as Jimmy's older brother and good friends with him, decided some form of retaliation was in order for my having put my new Hamilton name, and by extension his good name, in jeopardy. At least, that's the only reason I could think of for what happened next.

Shortly after I recovered from chicken pox, we set out to visit relatives. My mother's youngest sister, Jessie, had died of cancer of the liver soon after my arrival at the Hamiltons, and we were setting off to see how her widowed husband and their two boys, eight-year-old Leigh and one-year-old Dougie, were faring.

"Sharon, go fetch Billy so we can leave," said my mother, as we stood ready and waiting, "I think he might be out near the barn. And don't fall and get dirty." Twilight was already turning to dark, and I was more than a little afraid, first of the black shadow of the huge barn, and second that I might trip over something and dirty my dress.

"Billy, we're all waiting for you," I called, "Come on."

"Over here, Susie," I heard him whisper. "I've got something to show you."

"Where? Where are you? I can't see you. And why are you whispering?"

"I can see you. Just keep coming straight. That's right. Now stop right there and look straight ahead. Don't move."

I was inches from the open barn door, wondering what new mystery would be revealed and shivering slightly in the cool night air, when it hit. Like a bomb falling from the sky, a pointed fence picket lodged briefly in my skull, then fell blood-tipped to the ground. From the roof of the barn, directly overhead, one word pierced the night air, "Gotcha!"

My screams and bloodied dress kept us from visiting Leigh, Dougie, and Uncle Stan that night, and one week later Leigh was dead.

SEVENTH INNING STRETCH IN A FRIENDLY NEIGHBORHOOD BASE-ball game. Eight-year-old Leigh nibbling on a chocolate bar, unnoticed for the moment behind an empty grandstand. A sudden fierce gust of wind; grandstand topples; and Leigh is crushed to death. A few days later, Billy and I are sitting in the family car, waiting while our parents visit with relatives after the funeral. Billy's grief at losing his favorite cousin reveals a new aspect of his personality. He begins, through his tears, to talk of the times he and Leigh played together, then notices that I am not crying. I know I ought to cry. Everyone else has been crying for days. "A real tragedy," I heard over and over again. "Losing his mother so recently, and now dead himself. An innocent little child. An angel. Well, he'll be with God now. God takes back the best of us and makes us angels." An angel seems a nice thing to be. I hadn't ever met Leigh, but if God makes angels of the best of us, then from what I had heard, Leigh was already an angel in heaven. That doesn't seem too bad to me. But Billy is enraged. "You just don't understand, do you. You are alive and Leigh is dead. Nobody cares if you're alive, but we all loved Leigh. Don't you understand? Leigh is dead! We won't ever see him again. The least you can do is cry like everybody else."

I hesitate to reveal my stupidity, but manage to stammer, "I don't know dead. Tell me about being dead." Slap across my head. I see the next one coming and shield myself with my arms.

"I'll show you dead. And I'll show you how to behave when someone's dead. You cry when someone's dead. You don't talk about angels and shit like that. You cry. You cry because someone good is gone forever and someone like you is still alive. You cry, damn you, cry." And he swings at me and cries, and slaps me and cries, and punches me and cries, until I join him, both of us painfully crying for Leigh.

DEATH CONTINUED TO GRIP THE HAMILTONS THAT SUMMER, BUT the last death was closer to me than any of the others, strangely enabling me to understand Billy's cruelty engendered by his grief over Leigh. To help strengthen my legs, weakened by rickets, so that I could walk and run without falling down so often, a huge rope swing with a thick wooden seatboard was suspended from the sturdy branches of two large trees in our yard. The doctor believed that pumping the swing for an hour each day would help to develop the bones and muscles in my legs. Swinging alternated with running all around the farm with my new puppy, whom I named Sandy King.

Both the swing and Sandy King were part of my fourth birthday celebration. At least, the Hamiltons called it my fourth birthday. For me, it was my first. I couldn't believe all the glory heaped on a person just because they happened to have been born. Since I had never before had a birthday, and since mine coincided with Canada's birthday, I figured the

Hamiltons had just made it all up and had chosen a day that we could all remember fairly easily. In addition to giving me the swing and Sandy King, they built me a sandbox and bought me a bathing suit and two sundresses. Following only a few months after my first inundation of new clothes, such beneficence astounded me. But Sandy King and the swing were my favorites.

Sandy King and I each had one bad habit—well, actually I had a lot more than just one—that continually caused trouble. Sandy King's was sleeping in the middle of the road; mine was not being able to predict when my bladder needed emptying. One day, I got it right, but it ended up all wrong.

"I SWING THROUGH THE TREES WITH THE GREATEST OF EASE/ the dashing young girl on the flying trapeze," I sing loudly into the wind whipping through my hair. I love the rush of air with each stroke forward, and the slight feeling of imbalance with each swing back. I pump and pump to go higher and higher, Sandy King tracking each swoop of the swing, feinting little attacks whenever I near ground level. With clean face and clean overalls, breakfast comfortable in my tummy, morning sun kissing my cheek, my world is truly wonderful. Then I notice a slight pressure in the region of my tummy, and for the first time, I know how to read that pressure. I need to go to the bathroom. I don't want to, swinging so high, but I am also excited that I might be able to control this awful thing that makes everyone so angry at me all the time. I brake with my shoes, something I am not supposed to do because it scuffs the toes and makes them all muddy, and run to the house. Mom is in the bathroom, so I have to wait, urgently trying not to make a mess. Finally, it is my turn, and I dash in. I make it, and feel so good, so in control of myself, that I sit in there for a couple of minutes enjoying the possibility that I won't get into any more trouble about wetting myself. I know finally how to read the feeling. Mom's scream pierces my daydream, and I realize in an instant what has happened. The bathroom becomes a prison, and I dash out, but I don't know where to look and where not to look, so I cover my eyes and count to ten. When I finally dare to peer out, Mom is carrying the newspaper-wrapped bundle of Sandy King's remains off the highway into our driveway. "If I hadn't been in the bathroom, Sandy King would still be alive," is the thought that haunts me throughout the summer, and each time I go to the bathroom, I miss him dreadfully, and I worry about what other terrible thing might happen while I am in there.

MY PARENTS TRIED EVERYTHING TO STOP MY WETTING. IT BECAME an issue that invaded every aspect of my daily life. Billy could sit on Dad's knee; I couldn't, because he feared I might wet on him, even though I never did. Billy could cuddle up with Mom; I couldn't, because I was too often smelly and unclean. Billy could go on overnight visits and short trips; I couldn't, because I might wet the bed.

But even so, every morning, while I was still fresh and clean from my after-breakfast washup, Mom and I sat side by side on the chesterfield, and Mom read to me. Some of the stories were about little girls in families, and even though they got into scrapes, the stories always ended with the little girls being forgiven, and being held and hugged, and told that they were good little girls and that their Mommy and their Daddy loved them. One day, after swinging and thinking about the morning's story, I came inside to ask, "Why don't you ever hug me and call me *dear* or *my darling daughter* the way you always call Billy *dear* and *my darling son*? Don't you love me? You haven't ever told me you love me." I could tell from the look of surprise on Mom's face that she hadn't expected the question, hadn't realized the problem.

She looked at me, my overalls already darkened with the ever-present stain, and replied, "Well, with your pants always wet, and your temper tantrums all the time, you aren't very lovable, are you? You have to learn to smile." And then she broke into the refrain that she repeated every time I had a frown on my face:

> If I knew a box where the smiles were kept
> No matter how large the key/ Nor strong the bolt, I'd try so hard
> To make it open for me.
> Then over the land and sea broadcast/ I'd scatter the smiles to play
> That children's faces might hold them fast/ For many and many
>   a day.

Sometimes, when my sadness was too strong for a smile to subdue it, she continued to the next verse:

> If I knew a box that was large enough
> To hold all the frowns I meet/ I would try to gather them every one
> From nursery school and street/ Then closely and tightly I'd pack
>   them in/ And turning the monster key/ I'd hire a giant to drop
>   the box
> To the depths of the deep, deep sea.

By that time, I was so lost in images of boxes and giants and deep, deep seas that my frowns would have wiped themselves away.

But the thought that I was not lovable was difficult to deal with. I kept forgetting to smile. The black came almost every day, and when it did I screamed and raged and lashed out verbally and physically at everything and everyone around me. According to Mom, I was a whirling dervish always spinning and twirling or rocking, never able to sit or stand still. I was clumsy and fell more often than I should, I was always dirty and smelly, I sucked long strands of my hair and not just one but both thumbs, making them thick, flat, and misshapen from the pressure, I chewed open sores on my fingers and inside my mouth, and I caused problems everywhere we went. Terrified of being hit, I wouldn't go through a door if an adult were holding it for me and, when forced to, scurried through with head down, protected by my hands. Whenever anyone near me moved quickly, I jerked down, my hands shielding my head. I could tell that Mom and Dad were embarrassed, but I couldn't seem to control my reactions.

Also, Mom wanted a clean, polite, and sweet little girl to dress up and comb. I didn't measure up to any of those expectations. I was dressed and outside swinging before the rest of the family woke up. Faced with the intricacies of clothes that buttoned or fastened at the back, I put them on backwards and buttoned them up the front. By the time the others were up and eating breakfast, I was already dusty and dirty. Whenever Mom tried to help me get dressed or comb my hair, I shrank away and said, "I'll do it myself." I hated being scolded and responded either with a temper tantrum, a black rage, or a sullen scowl, and though I eventually learned not to swear audibly, I certainly vented my rage inwardly or under my breath with words "not fit for little girls to hear or say." In short, Mom was quite right: I was not lovable. What she did not seem to realize was how desperately I wanted to learn how to become lovable.

Though Billy was visibly loved, I could not see in him anything particularly lovable, other than that he never wet his pants and he laughed and smiled a lot, so I sought my models in the stories that Mom read to me. About five years later I finally discovered my role model in Lucy Maud Montgomery's *Anne of Green Gables,* but in the meantime I found snatches of personae with whom I could identify or from whom I could learn lessons and values. Johnny Appleseed showed me that I didn't need riches in order to be generous and helpful; that I should look around me to discover what is available to help others. Pandora, in the *Myths and Legends* Childcraft volume, was a natural for me to identify with, since she did the one thing she was told not to do. I also felt a close link to the little girl in one of my storybooks who, when she was good, she was very, very good, but when she was bad, she was very, very bad. And, in a similar vein, with the little donkey who, when he was glad, he was very, very glad, but when he was sad, he was very, very sad.

The story that kept me inspired and hopeful for years was "The Ugly Duckling." For me the story worked on several levels, because the "duckling"—the cygnet—was not a genetic part of the family to which she had attached herself and was inherently different in looks, personality, and even species. Most important, the cygnet had to wait until she was almost grown before she realized who she was and before others acknowledged the significance and grace of her difference. That whispered to the part of me that understood these readings at a deeper than conscious level not to expect any kind of quick transformation from the bad, ugly, smelly, and rude me that everyone saw to the good, pretty, clean, and gracious person I aspired to become. The major problem, and I consciously realized it even at the age of four or five, was that the transformation of cygnet to swan was natural, whereas my transformation would have to be learned. But then I used stories such as "The Little Engine That Could" to reassure me that my hopes were realizable. Every time I felt overwhelmed, I repeated over and over again, "I think I can, I think I can, I think I can."

Probably the greatest legacy from this early introduction to literacy was the notion—still below the conscious, articulate level, but nonetheless growing inside me—that if I could imagine or envision a reality beyond my own I would already be partway along the path to realizing that reality. The hard part—the part denied to those with no access to literacy—is realizing that other worlds exist and are accessible, though not without help, effort, and some good fortune. Those were the lessons of the myths, legends, and folktales of my childhood.

My books were not just pastimes; they were windows onto worlds inhabited by people who were governed by rules as whimsical as those in my real world. However, once I figured out the nature of the whimsy in my world of books, I could predict what would happen. That was more than I could do in my real world.

3

Be Good, Sweet Child, and Let Who Will Be Clever

Literacy has two beginnings: one, in the world, the other, in each person who learns to read and write. So literacy has two kinds of history: one, in the change and development over time of what **counts** *as literacy; the other in the life histories of those who learn to read and write, and who depend on these skills as features of their lives in literate societies. It is impossible to understand literacy without referring to its history, to those who are literate at any given time, and to what people actually* **do** *with reading and writing. So we have to unravel some of the meanings we give to literacy as a word, and some of the situations where we find it in use. This should help us to see more clearly what we understand about the nature of literacy nowadays, what we mean when we say we are literate, and why we are concerned about the literacy of our children.*

—M. Meek, *On Being Literate*, 13

7 he literacy of school and the literacy of schooling reflect contemporary beliefs, not just about learning but about societal values, especially in relation to the youth of society. This chapter shows the development of institutionalized literacy, the literacy of schooling that introduced me to societally validated models of what reading and writing and learning were all about during the early 1950s.

"WHY CAN'T I GO TO KINDERGARTEN? IF I GO TO KINDERGARTEN, I'll learn my numbers and learn how to read, so I won't be stupid when I go to grade one. The other kids on the street got to go to kindergarten. Why can't I?"

On and on I pleaded, as the rains fell ceaselessly that summer and fall of 1949. We had just moved to a new house built by my father in St. Vital, a growing municipality of Winnipeg, and at age five I was the only child over three years of age on my street not old enough to go to school. Kindergarten was not yet part of the public school system in St. Vital, but most of the other kids on the street had begun their schooling at Mrs. Willows' kindergarten class. Since Mom had not attended kindergarten and had never taught in a school system with a public kindergarten, she decided it was unnecessary. "It is more important for you to be outside running in the sunshine and strengthening your legs and lungs," she said.

Hearing that one of the neighbor kids had begun school while still five, I next tried that approach. I knew all my letters and numbers up to one hundred pretty well, and even though I still enjoyed being read to, I wanted the independence of being able to read by myself. Also, when the older kids on the street played school, they asked questions that I couldn't answer. I felt less able to play the game than the others, all of whom were already in school. I could spell pretty well and guess pretty well, but my actual knowledge about school matters was almost nil. The not-so-hidden curriculum in this neighborhood play school was that knowledge is power. I had no knowledge and therefore no power. School learning would give me both, I decided. But, despite my pleas, my one major failing prevailed. According to Mom, I couldn't go to school because at age five I still couldn't control my bladder.

IN EARLY SEPTEMBER, JUST A FEW WEEKS IN THE NEW HOUSE, I am playing outside dressed in clean white shorts and shirt, waiting for Mom so we can take our weekly walk to the Safeway supermarket eight blocks away. This walk is almost as good as our reading time, since it involves just the two of us doing something together rather than the two of us in confrontation over something I have done wrong. Unfortunately, in the five or ten minutes it takes Mom to get ready I have already wet my shorts and am sitting on the as yet unlandscaped ground of our new yard. I know I am in for trouble, but I don't anticipate the ensuing humiliation.

Examining my damp, soiled shorts, she says, "So, you want to go to school, do you? Well, let's go." Off we go, to the little four-room school just a block and a half away but on the other side of a very busy street. Nobody on our street, including my brother, goes to that school. Instead, they go to the big school—with nine grades and more than one room of each grade—that is six blocks away but on the same side of the busy street as our house. My request to let me change into something clean goes unheeded as Mom scolds, "Since you want to go to school so much, maybe this will cure you of your wetting." I don't understand the connection, since I have tried everything I can think of not to wet. My success the day Sandy King was killed recurs infrequently, and most of the time I have no warning that I can discern. But Mom and Dad have this notion that my wetting is deliberate, as though I want to cause them as much trouble as I can, and anything I say to the contrary is rebuffed with "Don't contradict me!" or worse, "If you can't behave, we'll take you back to the Greenhouse. How would you like that?" That threat effectively reduces me to sobs and promises but cannot change my inability to control my bladder.

We climb the stone steps of what had formerly been St. Vital's Municipal Hall and is now Fernwood School, grades one through four. Mom locates the principal's office, but since she is a teaching principal, we have to wait until recess while I absorb the smells and sounds of school. By the time the principal arrives, I have forgotten that my pants are wet and have actually begun to believe that she might decide to let me come to school. That hope is quickly dashed. After introductions, my mother comes immediately to the point, telling the principal how much I want to come to school; then she has me stand up and turn around. In shame, I do as I am told, then sink back as low as I can into my chair, hoping that by the time I come back for grade one next year, the principal, who will also be my grade one teacher, will have forgotten the entire episode.

EVEN THOUGH THE FORMAL ASPECTS OF LEARNING WERE BEYOND my reach for another year, Mom still read to me every day and, when the rain kept me indoors, gave me a box of alphabet letters, kept since her days as a country school teacher, to play with at the kitchen table.

They are cut-out cardboard squares, and I shake them onto the table and sort them into little piles. I then set the piles in order according to a Bing Crosby recording we have of the Alphabet Song, singing as I go: "A is for the apple that sits upon the tree; B is for the bird that sings for you and me; C is for the camel with two humps upon his back; D is for the duck that goes 'quack! quack! quack!' " I match the letters to anything I can find in the kitchen with print on it and then spell out my name. I also listen every morning to Kindergarten on the Air but am not very good at locating quickly enough all the stuff I need to do the activities—paste, paper, crayons, scissors, and so on—so mostly listen and sing along with the songs. It never occurs to me to gather all these items before the program starts. After Kindergarten on the Air is my reading time with Mom, followed ever since our move to the new house by a few minutes at the piano, since Mom considers me old enough to learn the notes and a few simple songs. The rest of the day is mostly spent getting into trouble.

Inside, there is not much to do, since I don't yet know how to read for myself, and I have played Snakes and Ladders, the only game we have, hundreds of times by myself. Sometimes I haul out our huge dictionary and let it fall open at the center, a colored insert the last page of which is covered with snakes, dominated in the middle by one huge rattler. I feel very brave sticking my finger into its open mouth, tingling with my fear and courage. Although at a conscious level I am secure in the knowledge that a picture cannot hurt me, something deeper inside me seems to acknowledge the power of the icon to create a verisimilitude. It is not a concept I can articulate, but it makes its presence felt emotionally, if not cognitively.

I don't spend all my time on bookish pursuits. I love getting into Dad's toolbox and building materials, and sawing, hammering, and painting any scraps of wood I can find lying about in the garage, hoping to impress Dad with my interest in building but always getting the same response: "Keep out of my tools. Hammering and sawing and painting are for boys and men, not for little girls. Besides, you could hurt yourself." For my fifth birthday, Mom gives me a doll with curly blonde hair and pink, frilly dress and bonnet, and I think the doll and I might become good play chums. Unfortunately, Mom catches me lifting up its dress and checking its bottom, which I have wet with water, and then spanking it harshly for wetting itself. "That's not the way to play with dolls," she scolds as she takes it away from me. It sits in her bedroom. I am allowed in every day to look at it but not to touch it until Mom decides I can play with it "properly." That day never comes. A few years later she gives the doll away.

So, when it rains, as it does so often this year, I mostly play with Mom's box of alphabet letters and look at the Childcraft books, not knowing whether I am actually reading them or just remembering the oft-heard words. I think of the world of the wraggle taggle gypsies, where the silk-gowned young lady runs off singing, "What care I for my house and land?/ What care I for my money, O?/ What care I for my new-wedded lord?/ I'm off with the wraggle taggle gypsies, O!" I wonder over and over how she could so easily give up all that I am sure I would find comfortable and desirable for a rough life with gypsies but am intrigued by the notion that there must be some sort of truth about life in the story somewhere. I am confused by the world of the Pirate Don Durk of Dundee. The poem begins, "Ho for the Pirate Don Durk of Dundee!/ He was wicked as wicked could be,/ But oh, he was perfectly gorgeous to see!/ The Pirate Don Durk of Dundee." The swashbuckling rhythms fascinate me, and I repeat the verses over and over, but the ethics are troubling. It seems to say that being wicked is not so bad if you are also gorgeous. The second-to-last verse makes that concept particularly vivid: "His conscience, of course, was crook'd like a squash,/ But both of his boots made a slickery slosh,/ And he went through the world with a wonderful swash,/ Did Pirate Don Durk of Dundee." He sounds splendid, and sometimes I think I could even be like the lady in the wraggle taggle gypsies and forsake my newfound comforts for his slickery sloshy life!

THESE WERE ONLY TWO OF THE MANY POEMS AND STORIES THAT were read to me and that I was beginning to read for myself (or remember and repeat to myself while looking at the print), but they stayed in my mind because they troubled me. They seemed to contradict the values and ethics I was supposed to follow, and they seemed to celebrate this contradiction. What was I supposed to believe? How was I supposed to behave? These books and stories were my only passports to worlds beyond my immediate neighborhood, and I was confused about the ethics and values in those other worlds.

Bit by bit, I determined that rules in the real world were intended to be followed absolutely—at least by children: always do this, never do that—whereas rules in my book world seemed to depend on who you were and what you wanted to achieve. I was already internalizing from these stories and poems the notion, bound to get me regularly into trouble, that rules are contingent, context-bound, and relative, made to be followed by those who couldn't think of a better way to get through life without bothering other people, at least, without getting caught. Several years later I was astonished to find, in *Of Human Bondage*, a renegade poet telling Philip, "Do what you want, but keep an eye out for the policeman around the corner." It seemed to confirm—and in my adolescent mind to validate—the morally slippery ethos I had been constructing from books and was beginning to apply in my real world.

I also came to the conclusion from these stories that I was "not human." My life was peopled not with tangible childhood friends but with fairies, gnomes, dwarfs, and legendary and mythical beings many of whom, like me, had no real parents and no history of their birth. As I mentioned before, the coincidence of my birth date with Canada's birth date and my lack of birthdays before coming to the Hamiltons had already thrown into doubt the idea that July 1 was really when I was born. I had no knowledge of my birth parents and thought that perhaps I didn't have any. When asked how I came to be born, my father told me I was found under a cabbage leaf. I didn't think it could be so, but again, his story did not tie me in directly with any other human beings. All the other kids I met had baby pictures and grammas and grampas, whereas I truly seemed to have sprung up in some unknown place at some unknown time.

So, being fascinated with the myths of the Immortals, I decided I was immortal. When I met book characters with yearning spirits imprisoned in imperfect bodies, I determined that my immortal spirit was imprisoned in a body made not of human skin but of pig skin, like the baby in *Alice in Wonderland* and like the tambourine my father had brought me from his most recent trip to the Caribbean. I caressed the tightly stretched skin of the tambourine, and it felt like my skin, so I began to worry I was growing too fast—the pigskin covering me would stretch and I would explode. This interior drama unfolded unspoken for several years, until at twelve my first menstrual period told me I was really human after all. At that moment of seeing the blood—which seemed intrinsically different from the blood of a gash or a scratch—I realized irrevocably that I was not made of pigskin, I was not immortal, and I would really die. Part of me was reluctant to relinquish a view of myself as exceptional, possibly because it had enabled me to justify my lack of friends among the regular human beings in my life. For the most part, however, I was relieved to discover that I must indeed be like other people.

But I am jumping too far ahead in the narrative.

OUTDOORS, DURING THE YEAR BEFORE I START SCHOOL, THE PO-tential for trouble is constant. Whenever the rains stop, I put on an old pair of Billy's rubber boots and test the puddles. The trick is to see how close to my boot tops I can let the water go before it comes inside, and of course the game does not end until I lose—much to my mother's dismay. One day I wander from my own as yet unfenced and ungrassed yard to a neighbor's equally muddy yard a few doors down. Unfortunately, the ground is so gooey that once my boots fill with water, they are sucked even more deeply into the rain-soaked Red River Valley muck than usual, and I can't get out. I pull and pull and howl and howl, but although several neighbors poke their heads out to see what my fussing is all about, no one ventures into the soggy sludge to help me out of my predicament. Finally, I realize that I will have to sacrifice the boots, and I pull my feet out, not relishing the idea of sticking them into the thick, gooey muck. To my surprise, after the first disgusting couple of steps, I begin to enjoy the squishy pull and arrive home with legs sculpted almost to the crotch in Red River gumbo.

That was the first time I realized that what might initially seem nasty or disgusting or negative might ultimately prove delightful. Even so, I always remember that it was a lot of work washing off that sticky goo.

The rains fell relentlessly, followed by a winter of record snowfall. By spring, the infamous flood of 1950 was upon us. I wrote about it eight years later in a school assignment, which I offer here as an example of my attempts to incorporate words from my eighth-grade vocabulary lists into written text and to recreate a sense of scene, as had been done so well, I felt, in the short story "The Most Dangerous Game." (I distinctly recall using the word *palpable* from "The Most Dangerous Game" because it seemed such an amazing descriptor for air. Added for this book is the reference to bedwetting, which I **never** would have mentioned at age thirteen.)

THE 1950 FLOOD
BY SHARON HAMILTON, NORBERRY SCHOOL, 1958

What I remember most about the 1950 flood is the night we were evacuated to Transcona and the day we returned to St. Vital.

Low-lying places all around us are already swirling with muddy pools, and the surge of the swollen river, a fraction below its already yielding banks, is tangible in the night air. Or perhaps the palpable fear comes instead from the urgency in Dad's voice: "You've got to get these kids out of here. The last train is leaving in less than an hour. By morning, this whole area will be covered with water."

Mom has just one request to make of Dad, a request she has voiced at least a dozen times over the past four days with no result. "Before we go, will you bring my trunk upstairs so that it's safe." Mom's trunk: the holder of treasures from her past; her three years in Africa in the late 1920s; her early years as a teacher in Birds Hill and Ashern; relics from her infancy in Lochinver, Scotland, from her girlhood in Transcona, and from the early days of her marriage in Baltimore; this history of her life in one cherished cache.

"Don't worry; I'll make sure it's safe," are the last words we hear as Dad bustles us through yet more rain into the taxi waiting to take us to the Canadian National Railway depot. We are not the only stragglers remaining two days after the official evacuation order, and the depot is a thronging madhouse. Like damp sardines, we are crammed into the train, so tightly packed that there is no danger of falling from the jolts as it shunts along the ten miles of track to Transcona. Many on the train will be at the mercy of volunteers willing to take strangers into their homes, but we are among the lucky who have relatives to stay with. Unfortunately, they don't have a car, and all the taxis are taken, so we have to walk the mile and a half to their house in the persistent night rain. Somebody at the station is handing out sections of newspaper to hold over our heads as we begin the long trek through the center of town, a parade of sodden evacuees. I stay with my Aunt Else and Uncle Stan and their three children, while Mom and Billy decide to head west for the Calgary Stampede. I can't go because of my bedwetting, which, naturally, annoys Aunt Else as much as it does Mom. Dad stays in Winnipeg to help with the cleanup. A few weeks later, we all arrive back to our home in St. Vital to find the signs of devastation, most notably the water scars on every home showing the height of the flooding, and here and there a stray toy or small piece of furniture, even the occasional bloated carcass of a small animal deposited in a lane or ditch and not yet spotted by the cleanup crews. But the worst view comes as we enter the house and see Mom's trunk, soddenly useless as a protector of her past, seeping sadly among the basement debris.

"Heigh ho, heigh ho, it's off to school I go," I sing over and over again until everyone is sick of hearing it. "Do you want to hear me count? How about the alphabet? A is for the apple that sits upon a tree; B is for the birds that sing for you and me; C is for . . . ." On and on I go, running up and down the stairs, making sure I have everything I might need. My new books smell of promise, and I have caressed them and my box of crayons, jar of paste, sleek pencils, and clean scribblers over and over again, with a kind of reverence for the knowledge they will help me gain. Mom has bought me two new school dresses and a new pair of shoes and has wrapped my hair in rags overnight so that it will curl into ringlets. I very quickly check my appearance in the mirror—something I rarely do since my Aunt Bella caught me looking at myself in the mirror one day and told me that if I did that too often I would come to fear my own reflection—and am satisfied.

My first lesson occurs in the playground before school even begins. I learn I have buckteeth and am therefore ugly. It is not yet a devastating discovery, since I have no idea that the epithet Buckteeth will haunt me for most of my school career. Mostly I wonder why no one in my family has ever mentioned it to me before. Then a girl with blonde, naturally curly hair and a pretty pink dress arrives, and I know she must be someone special because all the other girls run to say hello to her, and even the boys seem to find some excuse to walk close by. She reminds me, in a way that I can't explain but makes me feel uncomfortable, of the doll that I am not allowed to play with, still sitting in my mother's bedroom. She is so pretty and clean and popular, and I seem to know intuitively that I am not good enough to be friends with her.

Inside, some kids reply to their name with the word *here* and others with the word *present*. I decide, because it sounds nicer, that I will say *present* when I hear my name, even though no one seems to be getting anything that looks like a gift. But just before my name is called, a boy named Gerald Goodman is asked for more than a simple response. He has to spell his name ("Good," I think, "I can do that. I've been practicing all summer.") Then he is asked to spell his address. I am aghast. I can't do that. Nobody has told me that would be expected on the first day. I panic as the whisper hisses around the room, "He failed last year." My turn, and in my panic I founder, "Here, no, present." Someone in the class giggles, and I feel foolish already.

Then the teacher asks for volunteers to put numbers and letters on the board. This is the chance to rectify my initial clumsiness, because I have been practicing those numbers and letters for months. I am chosen for the number 4, and I am both excited and scared because that's the one that I sometimes start wrong and it often comes out looking like a chair more than a 4. Sure enough, at my first attempt, it looks like a chair, as several of my classmates point out in glee. I quickly erase it and start again, but I have forfeited my chance and am told to sit down and wait until I know what I am doing before I volunteer to share my knowledge with the class. I am bewildered. At home I just do it over until I get it right. At school I am expected to get it right immediately. I try to volunteer one more time, when we come to the letters, but the teacher does not choose me again.

After recess we are given pieces of blank newsprint to fold into neatly spaced lines: half over, then half over again, and then one more time. I am not a good folder, and my lines are all crooked. Again, there is no way to start over once the folds have creased the paper, so I ask for a new sheet of paper. The teacher is not pleased but gives it to me, and I begin the work but am briefly stopped when the teacher takes my pencil from what she calls my left hand and puts it firmly into what she calls my right hand. My mind is only partly focused on the lines and circles we are drawing onto the folded lines because, with the extra sheet of paper, I am already planning how to learn to spell my address by the afternoon. Just before lunch, we open our new readers, and then I am really excited. "By tonight, I'll be able to read the paper, just like Dad and Mom," I think. We learn Spot, Dick, Jane, Sally, run, look, and see in several variations, but it doesn't seem enough to get me reading the newspaper. As we leave for lunch, I slip my pencil into my pocket together with the badly folded sheet of paper. When I reach the corner of my street, I sit on the curb and copy the letters G-l-e-n-v-i-e-w A-v-e from the street sign. I say them over and over to myself, checking them against the paper, until I have memorized them. Then, as I walk up the front sidewalk to my house, I take note of the number, 15, which, for some reason, I had never noticed before, and spell it all again. Nobody asks me for that new bit of knowledge, but I feel better for knowing it.

"SO, HOW DO YOU LIKE IT IN THE BAD ROW?" I GLOWER IN RE-sponse, not fully knowing what the term *bad row* implies but intuitively realizing that my mother will not appreciate hearing about it. We are in LeMieux's, the corner grocery store, and Curtis, a boy from my class, is either just making conversation or trying to get me into trouble, I am not sure which.

"What's this?" my mother asks. "What's this about the 'bad row'?"

Curtis rushes to reply. "Sharon was just moved into the bad row, the row where all the kids are who can't do their work and who don't behave in class."

"We'll see about that," is my mother's only reply until we reach home. Then she demands, "Tell me more about the bad row."

A phone call and a day later I am moved again, this time to the row where all the good kids sit, including the pretty girl in pink, whose name I now know is Dorothy Penner. I decide I want to be just like her, nice and smart and well-behaved. It is impossible, and within a week I am in really serious trouble.

"Who stole Carol's milk?" rings out just after recess. Each morning, we give the teacher seven cents milk money for a pint of chocolate or white milk to drink at recess. The teacher counts the money, asks who wants chocolate and who wants white, and then writes the order on the blackboard for the milkman to fill when he comes later. Whereas most kids either always buy milk or never buy milk, my milk purchase is dependent upon whether my mother thinks I should have milk that day; sometimes she gives me the money and sometimes she doesn't. This recess I have just downed a pint of chocolate milk, thinking that I paid my seven cents during the morning collection. A quick check reveals otherwise.

"Sharon, stand up." I stand. "Class, you are looking at a thief, at someone who would steal from her own classmates. Sharon, sit down." I sit, and bury my head on my desk, not only because I am ashamed but also because I am so angry I want to blot everyone out. The teacher writes a letter to my mother and dismisses Carol fifteen minutes early so that she can deliver it to my home before I arrive for lunch, without fear of my beating her up on the way. She actually says that in the class. Nobody at school will look at me or talk to me.

When I arrive home, my place at the table is set with two quarts of milk, white milk. "Here, you love milk so much, drink this for your lunch."

"But it's chocolate milk that I really like," I protest, both furious and humiliated by all this fuss over what I consider to be a mistake, not a deliberate theft. My mother is also furious, threatening never to give me milk money again. I try to explain that if she would give me milk money every day, I wouldn't have to try to remember whether I had paid each day, but we argue over her view that I shouldn't drink so much anyway because then I'd have fewer wetting accidents. Though she does seem to understand that I did not deliberately steal the milk, she is unsuccessful in convincing my teacher. The upshot: no more milk money, which makes me look even guiltier among my classmates, most of whom have milk money every day.

NONETHELESS, I LOVED SCHOOL EVEN THOUGH I HAD NO FRIENDS. None of the kids lived on my side of St. Mary's Road, the main and therefore very busy street of the municipality, so the opportunity to make friends walking to and from school was limited. I was even more of a pariah in class after the milk episode, and that attitude extended, of course, to the playground, where if anyone called me thief or buckteeth I either laid into them with flailing fists or foul mouthed them into astonished silence. Of course, that behavior led directly to the strap, confinement in the cloakroom, or detention after school, during which I had to write a hundred times, "I will be a good girl." I neither wanted nor intended to get into trouble all the time, and I sometimes managed to stay out of it.

I learned to read very quickly but was not so quick at printing. I had difficulty remembering on which side to put the curvy bit in R and did it backwards as often as forwards, even though the letter is in my name and I should have been able to get it right. I confused *b* and *d* until I learned to make mental pictures of the word *dog* and the word *baby* and use them to help whenever I needed to print a word with *b* or *d* in it. N and Z also appeared backwards as often as forwards in my work, and the teacher still took my pencil whenever she saw it in my left hand and put it into my right. Suddenly, a few months into grade one, I automatically took the pencil into my right hand, knowing that it was my right hand and the proper place for my pencil, and within a few weeks of that event most of my letter confusion cleared up, and I just seemed to know, without having to figure it out, which way to print them.

ONE PARTICULAR DAY IN EARLY NOVEMBER OF GRADE THREE changes my entire orientation to school and to learning. I come in from recess to find my name on the board at the top of a list of ten other students: Sharon Hamilton, Brenda Harrison, Trudy Barton, Kathleen Mackenzie, Neil McKenzie. . . , my name with the names of the nicest and best kids in the class. What can this mean? What is going on? Whenever my name has been on the board before, it is because I have to stay in for doing something wrong. But these other kids on the list never do anything wrong. I stare and stare, wondering what it is all about, while all around me my classmates are abuzz. Then Miss McCruer, our teacher, announces that these are the top ten students in the class and that Brenda and I have tied for first place with the same average of 93.5 percent, but my name is at the top because my handwriting is better.

I find the whole business amazing. The previous year my handwriting grades ranged from poor to good, with an occasional very good, and I never quite figured out the reasons for the variation other than that the teacher wanted my letters made larger. This year the size of my letters seems to be fine, and the same handwriting, or so it seems to me, ranges from very good to excellent. And suddenly the teacher's phrase, "first in the class," rings a bell with me. At the end of grade two, Mrs. Frazer had given me a Winnie-the-Pooh book for "standing second in class." I had thought it referred to my place in the recess line, where I often had stood second, behind Dorothy Penner who usually stood first in line and who had received a book for standing first in class. For some reason, class standings have not been part of my awareness of school, maybe because they have never been written on the board before, or maybe because every one of my report cards so far has said some variation of "Sharon does good work but needs to talk less and to understand that the class rules are made for her to follow too."

I stare at my name and, for the first time in my life, feel special. The first in the class. It has a good ring to it; it sounds like something to be proud of, something my parents will be proud of. Maybe they will like me better, I hope.

While the class claps for the ten of us, I can't help but feel vindicated for my inauspicious beginning at this new school. I began grade three at Fernwood School, where I had been for grades one and two, determined not to get into my usual trouble, determined not to say a word unless spoken to. For the first week I was never spoken to; my name was never even called during roll call. I thought that odd but followed my resolution not to draw attention to myself in any way. When the second week began, and still my name hadn't been called, I thought I had better tell the teacher.

"Well, who are you? What is your name?" she demanded.

"Sharon Hamilton," I replied.

"Where do you live?" she asked. When I answered, she scoffed, "But that's on the other side of St. Mary's Road. You're supposed to go to Norberry School." By this time, the rest of the class was in hysterics, whispering, "She doesn't even know which school to go to."

"But I've been coming here for two years now. Nobody ever told me not to."

"Well, you're going to have to pack up your books and go to Norberry School. This school is for children who live on the east side of St. Mary's Road."

It seemed impossible. It had taken me three trips to school to get all my stuff here, and I had to pack it all into my arms and somehow walk five more blocks to the big school. And then it hit me. I would be going to the big school, to Norberry School, grades one to nine, where Billy was in grade eight. I stumbled into the sunlight, arms aching with books and supplies, and started up the road. My crayons fell first, then my new paints. By the time I reached Norberry, I was in a tearful rage at having dropped most of my stuff at least once, and at having skinned my knee on a piece of glass on the sidewalk as I knelt to pick up the fallen books and supplies. When I finally arrived, I was totally mystified. How was I supposed to open that huge door with all my books? Furious and frustrated, I kicked at the door with the heel of my shoe, and yelled, "Open the damn door. Open the goddamn door and let me in." It was a warm day, windows were open, and the door was quickly unlatched by an unsmiling teacher who ushered me immediately to the principal's office.

Mr. Wyatt had been expecting me, since the teacher had telephoned from the other school, but he hadn't been expecting me to have made the journey laden with a year's supply of books and school equipment. His kindness broke me into fresh tears, which he quickly brushed away as he took me by the hand to find me a classroom. "Sorry," said the first grade three teacher, Miss McCruer, "but all of the desks are full. There's no room."

"No room," a few kids echoed in whispers, and giggled.

So we tried the other grade three class but found the same problem. Every desk was taken. There was no place for me anywhere. Finally, Mr. Wyatt found me a desk from a grade five room and had it moved to Miss McCruer's grade three room, and I was settled in. But I knew no one, I was behind all the rest, and I felt the epitome of what Mom called a DP, a displaced person.

Now, seven weeks later, I am being honored by the teacher and my fellow students (at the teacher's command) for being first in class. It feels so good to have the teacher pleased with me and my classmates applauding me. I hope that some of them might even start liking me and be willing to be friends with me. At lunch, I run all the way home, breathless with my news. "That's nice," says my mother.

That's nice? That's all she can say? It's wonderful, I think, and I begin to build my first castle in the air. I will be first in class every reporting period.

IN MAKING THIS VOW, I WAS COMPLETELY UNAWARE THAT I was selling out my love of learning for an ephemeral label and setting myself up for continual failure, not to mention the increased contempt of my classmates. Even as I gradually became aware of the cost over the ensuing months and years, I counted it value for the price. Top marks became my goal and my solace; they were the only way I knew how to be special.

Reading was far and away my favorite subject, and I was distressed when in grade four it disappeared into a subject called literature. We began with a story of a little boy who wants to build a doghouse for Scotty, his loyal, playful Scottish terrier. He chooses the wood carefully, only the best will do, and decides to use screws, even though nails are easier and less expensive, because screws will make a longer-lasting, more securely built home for his precious pet. I learned from that story that when someone or something is important to me, I should give my very best effort to whatever I make or do for that person or animal. But the teacher didn't ask about that. Instead, she passed out paper and we had a test. What is the boy's name? Timmy or Tommy or some such; I hadn't paid attention to that because it hadn't seemed important. He was not real to me; only the principle that made him build the best doghouse he could was real to me. How many days did it take to build the doghouse? I hadn't bothered to remember that either. What kind of dog will live in the house? That was easy. Dogs were important to me, and hadn't seen a Scottish terrier before, so I had paid attention to that. Who wrote the story? I thought, Who cares? and left another blank. In all, I answered four out of ten correctly, which was not likely to put me in first place. So I came to the conclusion that literature is remembering authors and details, and I put my attention to that, in the process losing a bit of my joy in reading. I was ready for the next test, however, and made certain to get ten out of ten.

High grades spun me into a world of unreality—isolated and only seemingly controllable. Anything below 90 percent I bemoaned as failure, believing my father utterly when he said, "If you can get 99, you can get 100. Just try a little harder." I was blind to my obsession or rather preferred to see it as a valued part of my existence, the one place I could shine and be special. My mother gave me an autograph book just before my tenth birthday, inscribing its first page, "Be good, sweet child, and let who will be clever." My grade five teacher, on the last day of school, wrote a verse from Kipling in it: "If you stop to consider the work you have done/ And to boast what your labor is worth, dear/ Angels may come for you, Willis, my son/ But you'll never be wanted on earth, dear."

But that same grade five teacher introduced me to another obsession even more powerful than a straightforward addiction to high grades. She read to us *Anne of Green Gables*, and Anne became my alter ego, my role model, my exemplar of values. Being like Anne became my preoccupation. In the middle of the twentieth century I tried to redefine and re-create myself as a late-nineteenth-century orphan, initially not wanted but despite many setbacks eventually proving her worth to her new caregivers and their community. Anne proved her worth, in my perspective, by sticking to views and values that were different from many in the community and by winning scholarships to university, and she grew up to be beautiful and loved. I was determined: so would I.

4

It's a Good Thing You Don't Wear Glasses

What is certain is that we now extend the idea of "being literate" to other areas of our lives which have no direct connection with reading and writing the language we speak.

—M. Meek, *On Being Literate*, 38

*T*he English teacher in me wants to respond to the statement in the epigraph with the view that once we have learned to read and to write, what we read and write connects, at least indirectly, with everything else we do. It is a way of agreeing with Margaret Meek's observation that what we consider literacy goes far beyond the acts of reading and writing. Our literacy encounters provide not just a stockpile of knowledge and skills to be tapped and utilized but also—at least equally important—a reservoir of vicarious experiences that can prepare us emotionally and intellectually for unforeseen or unpredictable situations. This chapter, which begins in a sordid nightclub, ventures into shoplifting and lying, strays too close for comfort to prostitution, confronts the teachings of religion, and moves from one unforeseen or unpredictable or socially deviant situation to another. In each situation, Meek's notion of extended literacy is evident as I draw on and build my reservoir of experience.

"LADIES AND GENTLEMEN, THE BON VIVANT IS PROUD TO PRE-sent the lovely and talented Christina and her show, The Evolution of Female Accomplishment."

To the applause of a full house, I maneuver my ornate satin gown between crowded tables to take my place at the piano. Devotees of the Bon Vivant, anticipating the customary belly dancer or torch song vocalist to embellish their cocktails, dinner, and later entertainments, instead hear me playing the restrained harmonies of a Kuhlau sonatina. After the final chord I make a slight costume adjustment and move through the crowd with bustle and parasol to the previously taped strains of a Strauss waltz. The parasol collapses into a cane, and I hop onto the piano bench and tap dance to "Give me that old soft shoe." I leap off the bench, turn around once, and bustle and parasol fall away to reveal the tassel-fringed shift of the roaring twenties. I wriggle into the Charleston to the strains of "If it's naughty to rouge your lips, shake your shoulders, and shake your hips, well, then, baby, I wanna be bad!" Saxophone-smooth "Chicago, Chicago" announces the dirty thirties, and fringed tassels, conveniently attached to my flapper shift with Velcro, become baby boas to tickle customers with as I perform a Prohibition-era bump and grind from table to table. Exhausted and dripping perspiration, I return to the piano to play the sentimental forties tune "Suddenly There's a Valley," then Elvis' lively "Don't Be Cruel." I then slink into my main dance number, the provocative if not very subtle "You Give Me Fever." By this time, I am clothed in a pink satin body suit and fishnet tights, fully appropriate for "Peppermint Twist," the closing number of my twenty-five-minute show.

I am nineteen years of age, dancing in a nightclub that fronts for a prostitution ring—although I hadn't known that when I accepted the job—and teaching by day in a one-room eight-grade country school fifteen miles south of the city. Anne of Green Gables by day, and the closest I can come to being sexy and desirable at night. Every performance, as I hear the appreciative comments of the customers, I think of one of the last comments made by my father before he turned his annual three-month winter vacation into almost permanent absence.

I WAS THIRTEEN AND SKINNY, WITH LONG, OILY HAIR, PIMPLY skin, distorted rib cage that protruded more than my flat chest, braces, and huge, clumsy hands and feet, utterly miserable with my newest isolating nickname at school, Cooties. I rarely complained at home about feelings of rejection at school, because, whenever I did, my mother, who had grown up in times more similar than mine to those of Anne of Green Gables, would offer me one of three formulaic phrases as a response to the tormentors. The first is familiar to almost every child, who intuitively knows the lie it tells: "Just reply, 'Sticks and stones may break my bones/ but names will never hurt me.'" The second I have never heard from anyone but my mother, but it is equally unhelpful: "Just nod your head [she would cock her head to the right, the left, and back to center] and say, 'oh! oh! oh!'" Even in my social ignorance, I could imagine the hoots that would follow that response. Her third rejoinder came most often when I complained that she, rather than my classmates, had hurt my feelings: "fee . . ee . . lings," she would reply, with drawn-out emphasis, "fee . . ee . . lings! Who has time for fee . . ee . . lings? Nobody ever worried about feelings when I was growing up. You don't need feelings. If you feel so bad, go look at the children with no arms and no legs at the Shriners Hospital. Then you'll feel lucky. Why can't you be like Topsy? Topsy had no feelings. She just grew." Poor little Topsy, in Harriet Beecher Stowe's *Uncle Tom's Cabin*, had feelings aplenty, I'm sure, but any reply would be labeled "contradicting," so I just stopped telling although couldn't stop feeling.

There we were, at the family table for lunch, the air tense between my mother and my father, though I was so lost in my own misery that my only acknowledgment of their tension was staying quiet myself. Then Dad looked at me, looked almost straight through me. I wondered what he was thinking.

"It's a good thing you don't wear glasses," he said.

"What? Why?"

"You have no sense of how a young girl should look. Look at yourself! Your hair is a mess, you still have braces on your teeth, you're too skinny, you have no idea how to dress, and you have pimples all over your face. Don't you have any notion of how to groom yourself? And you smell. How often do you bathe? No man is ever going to look at you or want to date you." And then he turned on Mom: "What's the matter with you, Kit? Can't you make her learn how to look after herself properly?" A week later he was gone, though he was gone so often that it was almost a year before I realized that he might not be coming back. Even then, it was my next-door neighbor, in response to my vague speculation that it was about time Dad was returning, who jolted me to consciousness: "Sharon, your dad's been gone a whole year. He's left your mother. Didn't you know?"

"CHRISTINA," CALLS MEL, ONE OF THE CO-OWNERS OF THE BON Vivant, "you've been invited to join a table for between-show drinks." I put away the student papers I have been trying to read in my dressing area between performances, doff my after-shower robe, and don my party dress, hoping the waitress will remember that I am not allowed alcohol in my drinks; it reacts with the phenobarbital I am taking for an incipient ulcer. The fact that I am under twenty-one, the legal drinking age, no longer seems relevant.

"Good evening," I smile as I join the table, vaguely aware that I have seen these faces before. And then I realize they are all members of my school board, the trustees of education and moral guidance for the students I teach. The advertisement for my show has been brought to their attention, the picture sufficiently accurate to nullify my stage name disguise as Christina, and they have come to ascertain whether I am violating the letter or spirit of my contract, offered to me primarily because my handwriting had been the best of all the applicants. Although I as yet have little respect for myself as a teacher, I do have respect for my contract and for the concerns of these men. "The show, we are happy—and relieved—to say, is not a problem," they assure me. "We are only worried that you won't be able to devote full attention to your teaching duties."

I think of the still unread assignments in my dressing area and inwardly agree. "Oh, you needn't worry," I reassure them. "I have plenty of time between shows, and my ride drops me at school almost an hour before starting time and doesn't pick me up until an hour and a half after we're done for the day. I've lots of time to get most of my preparation done." They seem satisfied. I am not.

MY TINY SCHOOL SAT SQUAT IN THE MIDDLE OF A SWEEPING prairie landscape. Soon I would be able to pump water again from the spring well beside the school, but in these frigid winter months our daily supply of water was dropped off in a huge plastic bottle by a parent when he dropped off his nine-year-old son. There was just one room, with a small divider for the furnace. Every day eighteen children—three in grade one, two in grade two, three in grade three, four in grade four, three in grade five, one in grade six, one in grade seven, and one in grade eight—helped me teach them how to learn.

"I'll show you the ropes," fifth-grader Cathy had volunteered, her wide blue eyes taking in my unfamiliarity with eight grades in one small room. And with generous, efficient dispatch, she did. We soon had everyone either learning or helping someone else learn, and the classroom began to hum with activity. Having vicariously lived through Anne of Green Gable's days as a student and then as a teacher in her tiny one-room eight-grade school in Avonlea, I had been able to envision, at least in part, my role in that otherwise foreign atmosphere. My literacy experiences with Anne had helped to introduce me to a world as new to me as the one my six-year olds were encountering with their introduction to reading and writing. And, although I didn't realize it at the time, these experiences were forming the foundation for how I would later view teaching and learning. This first year of teaching had slam-dunked me into the basket of collaborative learning, not yet as a theoretical perspective on how knowledge is constructed but as a pragmatic necessity for getting through the school day.

Despite the correspondence of my first teaching situation with that of Anne of Green Gables, it was not what I had envisioned for myself. When I was eight and nine, my shortcut to school through the grounds of derelict greenhouses would cross the route of the daughter of my fourth-grade teacher, on her way to catch the bus that would take her to the University of Winnipeg. One day she saw me crying and stopped to talk with me, starting up a friendship that lasted, during the few daily moments that our paths crossed, for the next two years. She was studying English, and her books looked fascinating. I asked her all sorts of questions about university and went home one day to announce to my mother that I was going to have my B.A. in English by the time I was twenty, my M.A. at twenty-two, and my Ph.D. at twenty-four. Then I would become a professor of English at the University of Manitoba. It sounded wonderful to me, a job doing every day what I already loved doing, reading books and writing. It did not sound so wonderful to my mother, not when I was eight and even less when I was eighteen.

"A woman must be independent, able to earn her own living. You don't ever want to be economically dependent upon a man so that you can't go your own way when you want to. You can have one year of either a business college or a teachers college when you've finished grade twelve. Then you'll have a starting point, a license and a career that you can always fall back on." What she didn't say then but years later told me had weighed equally strong in her decision was that knowing how much I wanted to be loved by someone and how unloved I felt, she feared I would fall for the first man interested in me and get pregnant without any means of supporting myself.

"Why didn't you simply love me then?" I wanted to ask, to cry out almost in accusation, but she was over eighty when she confessed her underlying motivation, and there was no point in upsetting our finally flourishing camaraderie and trust. Only recently, since I have begun writing this book and sharing the manuscript with her, have I realized that she was asking an equally unspoken, equally anguished question: "Why didn't you simply realize you *were* loved?"

SO, THINKING THAT A TEACHERS COLLEGE WAS A STEP CLOSER TO university than a business college, I chose the former and began my teaching career as a prairie schoolmarm.

My short career as a nightclub dancer came about even more oddly. With ten years of dancing lessons, I had auditioned the summer after Teachers College for *West Side Story* at Rainbow Stage, Winnipeg's outdoor theater. When my number was called, I jumped onto the stage in plain black leotard and tights, and earned a spot in the chorus with my interpretation of "You Give Me Fever." Word of my audition entered the pipeline of nightclub owners. A few months later I was called and asked to expand my audition routine to a twenty-five-minute show for the Bon Vivant. I was flattered. Ugly me, the kid with no friends, the kid with buckteeth, the Cooties of the class, would be on stage, the center of attention, sexy and desirable: the proposition was irresistible.

My mother's response was based on economics: "Well, it's about time you get some return for all the money we've spent on dancing lessons. Sounds like a good idea to me, if you can keep up with your teaching." My boyfriend's response was the clincher: "If you dance there, with all those men ogling you, you can just say good-bye to me. It's evil; it's wrong; it's immoral." I found those words preposterous, a denunciation of years of lessons and recitals that in my perspective were just as acceptable as the Bach and Beethoven and Mozart that I performed at my piano lessons and recitals.

And yet, at that time, Robert, whom I had met at Teachers College, was more important to me than any man had ever been. While I was teaching in my one-room prairie schoolhouse, he was teaching up north on a remote Indian reservation, and we saw each other only every second weekend. Every night and every other weekend I stayed at home, knitting him an intricately patterned Mary Maxim sweater, chamois-lined to keep him warm, while my mother urged me to be out dating others and having fun. I saw myself as loyal and loving, and I saw my dancing as an extension of a harmless activity that I had done all my life. Angered at his response, at his definition of me as cheap and untrustworthy, as though dancing at the Bon Vivant would somehow change the essence of who I was, I made up my mind to take the job.

"CHRISTINA," MEL INTERRUPTS MY REVERIE. "THERE'S A FELLOW here with a proposition for you to consider."

"You mean you are offering me a dance circuit in nightclubs across the United States?" I ask in astonished disbelief. As though out of a Hollywood B film, the paunchy man across from me draws deeply upon his cigar and blows out the smoke in one long smooth stream, punctuated by a series of rings at the end. He has just spent fifteen minutes describing the life of an exotic dancer, telling me how well he treats his girls and how I will have guaranteed employment for the next four months. In reply to my comment that I already have guaranteed employment right now with my teaching contract, he tells me that I can earn "big bucks," depending upon how I redesign my routine—and costume.

Thinking of my distorted rib cage, with distended lower ribs and pulled in sternum, resulting in a hole large enough to fit an orange in my almost flat chest, I applaud the cleverness of Mallabar's costume design department in camouflaging all these physical deficiencies so successfully. I actually consider the offer, mostly because of the money, but recognize that good facial bone structure will take me only so far. I simply do not have enough flesh in the right places to make it as an exotic dancer. Morality has a negligible role in my decision. In the contest of physical assets versus mental assets, my body loses, and I tell the man an easy no.

But I am intrigued by the offer after so many years of feeling unattractive—*ugless* I used to call it, not even sufficiently interesting to be ugly—and by the idea that people would find me seductive and alluring. My value on myself is so low that I am more flattered than offended the first few times I am propositioned by the patrons. Someone wants to make love to me and even pay me for it. It seems a strange bargain, where I win both ways. I stand firmly in my no, again not through moral qualms but because I think that just as I ought to have a good mind in order to develop the minds of my students, I should have a good body if I expect to be paid for sharing it with someone. And, in my perspective, I don't.

I do agree, however, to be a party girl one night. I don't know what that entails, but the advance pay is very good. With movie-induced visions of charming men, champagne cocktails, and elegant surroundings, I carefully choose a close-fitting royal blue dress and brush my long dark hair until it shines. I arrive ready to dance and have some fun, and am told to "get naked." The shadows of six men suddenly assume clear focus, and I realize in an instant that I am in trouble. "The other girl couldn't make it, so it's just you, honey. You're going to be one busy little lady, so hop to it."

"I can't make it either, actually. I'm just here to return your money," I improvise as I forage in my purse. The man in charge locks the door, knocks my purse onto the floor, and clamps his paws onto my shoulders.

"Now you listen to me, you little tramp. I hired you to give my boys a bit of fun, and I expect you to do just that. This here's our annual little get-together, something I do for my boys every year, to keep them happy, little present to keep up their morale. So you just bare that little tush and get into that room and I'll send them in one at a time. Then you can come out and do a little dance for us, and we'll start all over again."

My mind races, trying to find a way out. And then I remember Bonnie, one of the hostesses at the Bon Vivant, bemoaning the fact that she had to take six weeks off from hooking because she was infected and might infect her customers. Actually, she was bemoaning the loss of income while celebrating the loss of input. I figure out my ploy just as he orders me into the bedroom.

"Look, I hate to disappoint you, but I'll bet you're not ready or wanting to be crippled from syphilis." And I show him the row of open sores just inside my mouth, caused by my nervously biting my lip, a habit I've had since childhood, but he doesn't know that. "And it's worse down here," I tell him. "That's why I've come to return your money. My doctor just gave me a shot yesterday (thank heavens for my education from the Bon Vivant hostesses) and forbade any sexual contact whatsoever for the next six weeks." And then I look straight at the youngest-looking man, whose furrowed brow makes him seem the most miserable being there, and plead, "I'm sorry. I'm really sorry." Then I fall to my knees, hoping desperately that these rapid shifts of mood and statement will unnerve at least one of them sufficiently to suggest letting me go. And even in the terrible poignancy of the moment I feel like three people: one, the terrified and repentant slut, fallen angel on the floor; one looking at the whole scene in disgust, wondering at the stupidity that got me into this mess; and one actually, unbelievably, applauding my spontaneous dramatic performance.

A kick in the ribs, in my stomach, coming at my head, and I roll over, while the sad-looking fellow finally decides to hold off his boss. The others stand bewildered as I shakily regain my feet and pick up my purse. The cheerless young man unlocks the door for me and gently touches my shoulder as I leave, the foul imprecations of his boss ringing in my ears for days following.

I GAVE MY NOTICE AT THE BON VIVANT AND ENDED MY FLIRTATION with show business. In so doing, I marked another stage in my definition of self. I knew I was not a tramp, not a whore, not an exotic dancer, even as I also knew, from talking and working with prostitutes for six weeks, that the women who lived these lives were not less honorable than I was. Circumstances, not always of their own making, had forced them to make difficult choices for themselves, often more justifiable than the choice that had led me into that almost disastrous situation. It was one of those moments when I realized, not retrospectively but right at the instant, how luck and mental agility can interact to guide our entire existence. That event and my life could easily have turned out otherwise.

Flirting with the shady side of society's rules and mores was not new to me. Having been designated a bad apple, a liar, and a thief long before I was actually or at least consciously guilty of these crimes, I had not found it a huge step into the realm of acting them out. Much of how we define ourselves is shaped by how we are defined by others, and I had been defined as "bad" over and over again.

My first deliberate theft came soon after the school milk episode. My brother, four and a half years older, had been receiving an allowance ever since we had moved into the city and lived near places where money could be spent. From his allowance he had managed to save four quarters, which Mom kept in a little box exactly the size of the four quarters framed in its interior. These she showed with pride to everyone who visited the house. "Look at what Billy has done. He has saved these four quarters." Jealousy gnawed at me every time Mom showed off the coins and praised Billy. I didn't really need money, since I hadn't ever had any and so had no idea what it was like to buy myself something, but I nonetheless decided to steal one of the quarters, leaving a gap in that perfect symmetry of goodness. Of course the theft was soon discovered and of course I was the one suspected and of course I foolishly had hidden the coin in my drawer where it was easily found.

That act had three results. The first was that Dad decided an allowance would be a good way to teach me the value of money and of other people's possessions, and he began to give me a dime a week. The second was that Billy, understandably, needed to get even. One evening soon after, he was left babysitting me, and was furious because he wanted to go out with his friends. To keep me from getting into any trouble while he went out, specifically to prevent me from taking any more of his things, he forced me to lie with my face on my bed, tied my hands behind my back, jerked up my ankles and tied them to my hands, and then put the last bit of rope around my neck, so that if I moved, I'd strangle. I don't remember how long he left me like that, but our parents arrived home before he did, and untied me, stiff, weak, and unable to move a muscle. They did not say very much, either to me or to Billy, at least that I overheard, and the only acknowledgment of the danger to my life came a couple of years later, when Dad tried to bring Mom into the second half of the twentieth century with the purchase of a dishwasher, an automatic washer and dryer, and a deep freeze. Mom sent them all back to the store, saying, "I've got a dishwasher, a ten-year old female one, and I don't need a washer and dryer when Peerless will pick up my laundry and do it for me, and we can't have a deep freeze; Billy's likely to put Sharon inside and leave her there." The third result was that stealing became an activity I learned to excel at.

"REVEREND HENDERSON, CAN YOU HELP ME? YOUR SERMON LAST Sunday spoke of an inner guiding sense of what is right and what is wrong. I don't think I have that inner guiding sense, or, if I do, I'm ignoring it. What should I do?"

I am sixteen, and I am shoplifting clothes from Eaton's as often as once a month. I know it is wrong in the legal sense, and I know it is wrong in the spiritual sense, but it seems a more or less fair equalization of property in the very real sense of the world I live in—or at least it does at the time of the stealing. Afterwards, I have a difficult time reconciling what I have done—what I continue to do—with the person I want to become. Anne of Green Gables would never steal. But I do. And I do not have a problem reconciling the thefts with my view of the world's morality, which I had already begun questioning, as I mentioned earlier, when reading about Robin Hood and the Pirate Don Durk of Dundee. I have long ago learned that people profess morality more than they carry through on it, and that the adults who exhort me, punish me, teach me, and otherwise influence my life often lose their own struggles with right and wrong. I had recognized immediately the incongruity of my father's telling me at age five not to lie, because whenever I did, he said, a red light came on in my eye. Even realizing years later that the "red light" was his way of telling me that the look in my eyes gave the lie away, I could not shake my initial impression: "He's lying to me while telling me that lying is wrong."

But Reverend Henderson is not impressed with my rationalizations. "What about the Ten Commandments? What about the laws of the land?" he asks.

"The Ten Commandments are unrealistic," I respond. "They don't take into account human nature. 'Thou shalt not covet!' Everyone I know covets something that belongs to someone else."

"Well," he sighs, "if the Ten Commandments aren't good enough for you, then what about the laws of the land?"

"Nobody pays attention to them unless they're forced to," I reply, wondering why he doesn't realize that I have already thought all this through or I wouldn't have come to him in the first place. "Almost every adult I know tries to get away with paying less tax than they are supposed to. And will speed and then lie to avoid a ticket. Laws are just general guidelines for society's overall benefit. They don't help with individual decisions."

"Like what?"

"Like how far I should go with my boyfriend. Like whether I can be cheeky to an adult who has been cheeky to me. Like whether I have to return extra change if the cashier thinks I've given her a ten instead of a five. Like . . ."

"Not, no, and yes. Now how difficult was that?"

"No, it's more complicated than that. I mean, is there a way I can develop a personal set of standards or rules that is just right for me and that I can use when I need to make a decision instead of sorting through each crisis in my life and trying to figure it out all by myself every time?"

"Little lady, if the Ten Commandments aren't good enough for you, and the laws of the land aren't good enough for you, then I can't help you. Now, I have some people waiting who really need my time, so why don't you just do what you're supposed to do, and stop fussing about what you don't need to fuss about."

I feel so humiliated, so put down, that I catch the downtown bus right outside the church, get off at Eaton's, and steal a beautiful Italian knit suit I noticed a week earlier, priced at over two hundred dollars, careless, almost daring the saleslady to catch me, probably the most potentially self-destructive shoplifting spree I have ever engaged in. Luck overbalances mental acuity (or, in this case, lack of it), and I get away with it. Nonetheless, it turns out to be the last time I steal anything.

"Sharon, I want to talk to you," my mother says. "When I was at Eaton's yesterday, I saw a suit like the one you said you bought last week for fifty dollars. It's two hundred and fifty dollars! And that's not all. I checked through your closet, and saw suits and dresses that you can't possibly afford on what you earn working weekends. I want some answers and I want them now, or I'm calling the police. If you've stolen them, I'm calling the police anyway. You remember that story I always told you about the mother and her thieving son."

Indeed I do. The day my theft of Billy's quarter was discovered was the first time I heard it, but in the intervening ten years I have heard it at least a dozen times more. A little boy brings home a ball that he has found, and his mother asks him where he got it. He says, "I just found it," and his mother lets him keep it. Next it's a bicycle, and then a motorcycle, and then a car, and on it goes until the boy becomes a man about to be hanged for killing someone during an armed robbery. His mother begs to see him, and finally he consents. As she throws her arms around him, he bites off her nose, saying, "That's for not punishing me for stealing the first time, when I brought home that ball."

My mother's message is clear. Unlike her earlier threats to return me to the Greenhouse, these threats to call the police are real. I lie in bed, sorting through it all, trying to figure how I can extricate myself from this mess, vowing that if I do, I will never steal again. As a teenager who regularly attends church and church-related youth groups, I generally subscribe to the notion that truth, at least some version of it, is the best defense. However, in this case, Mom has made it clear that the truth will result in a visit from the police. From time to time in my stealing escapades, I have thought I almost wanted to get caught, but now, threatened with the reality of jail, I am terrified. My breath begins to come in shorter and shorter spurts, and almost without realizing it, I start to whimper. The plan flashes into my head, and I deliberately begin to escalate my whimpering. Eventually it intensifies to a wail of terror, and Mom calls out, "What's wrong?"

I run downstairs and fling myself into her bedroom. "I'm scared and I can't tell you why. Just don't call the police tomorrow, or I'll be in worse trouble than you can imagine."

"What do you mean?"

With feigned reluctance, I slowly allow Mom to drag the story out of me. "Well, you know I like to go to the Java Shop to watch the people all in black, smoking their sweet-smelling cigarettes, looking terribly cool and sophisticated sipping espresso or cappuccino. Anyway, a few months ago, I met a group of people. They run a shoplifting ring, taking turns distracting salesclerks and stealing clothes, then bootlegging them at the Java Shop. They've sold stuff to me, that's how I get it so cheap, but they told me that if I ever ratted on them, I'd be dead meat."

"Look. I can't tell whether you're lying or not, but I will say this to you, and I will say it once only. If I ever see another dress or suit in your closet that I know you haven't bought with your own money, I'm calling the police. That's my last word on it. We will not talk about this again."

We don't. But the threat of calling the police wakes me up to several realizations. First, I obviously value my life in the free world more than I thought I did; second, I hate the burden of lying that goes along with stealing; and third, I do not like thinking of myself as a thief. The upshot is that I keep my vow never to steal again, and I imagine myself a snake shedding its old, dirty skin, and finding myself clean and fresh, lighter by a feather-weight, but infinitely purer. I am worthy of Anne of Green Gables, or at least becoming so.

5

Lying in the Bed I Made

THE '60S PASSED ME BY

The most strongly held and the most lasting conviction about the importance of being literate rests on the belief that by learning to read and write we can all read and write to learn. This is not a foolish idea. The lives we lead are the result of its implications.

—M. Meek, *On Being Literate*, 165

The fundamental premise of the literacy narrative is that by reading about the lives and ideas of others, we can begin to question and reshape our own lives and ideas. By writing about our lives, particularly in relation to the lives of those close to us, we unconsciously make connections as we journey through our memories and impressions. When articulated in our writing, these connections become stepping stones in the rivers of our reading and through the forest of our experience. These stepping stones connect ideas and events, and guide our efforts to refine and redefine our lives. This chapter highlights a critical moment when reading and writing to learn completely changed my orientation to myself, my marriage, and the possibilities engendered by intellectual growth.

"HOW CAN YOU HAVE LIVED THROUGH THE SIXTIES AND NOT know anything about the music or the culture?" my son asks me from time to time. The decade of the Beatles, the Kennedys, the peace movement, and unprecedented research and development in medicine, science, technology, and general education should also have been the decade of my intellectual awakening, of the "flowering of my young womanhood." Those who believe that there is such a period in a woman's life usually characterize the ages from sixteen to twenty-five as that idealized time of discovery and exploration. In retrospect, I see choices that I did not realize I had. At the time, I felt channeled, actually more like eddied, into currents that simultaneously re-sisted and reflected the social and moral code for women at that time. In re-creating this portion of my life, I have difficulty with the self-centered, socially inept woman-child who emerges in all the scenes that flash through my mind. Part of me wants to hold her and stroke her hair and tell her, "It's okay, you did the best you could, all things considered." Another part of me wants to grasp her by the shoulders and shake her and say. . . . Well, what do you say to a child becoming woman who thinks she knows it all and really knows almost nothing worthwhile?

As part of my preparation for writing this narrative, I asked Olga Kruk, one of my teachers in high school, what general impression she had had of me during my high school years. She replied that she could sum it up in one word: *sad.* She went on, "You had a sadness about you that seemed too old in one so young."

"WELL, MOM, WHAT DID MY TEACHERS SAY?" I ASK WHEN MY mother comes home from parents' night at the high school.

It is 1961, two months into my grade twelve year, and I am president of the drama club, co-editor of the school newspaper, working on the yearbook staff, and hoping to earn a scholarship to university. My extra-curricular status has been gained through desire (mine) and by default (of others equally or more capable), not through popularity. I am still a social washout.

Mom believes a girl should know about her body and about cooking, cleaning, and sewing, and therefore insists that I take biology and home economics rather than French, Latin, chemistry, and physics, which my university-bound classmates are taking. I manage to wriggle out of home economics and am able, without her signature, to schedule French and Latin in addition to biology, and so still have some university options open to me.

"Well, I was never so humiliated in all my life," answers Mom. "What do you do all day? Just talk to your teachers? That Roslycky woman, what's her name, Kruk now? told me that she can't turn around without you bothering her all the time. Mr. Hryhor tells me you are doing nothing in math, and all the other teachers say you are just prancing off to extracurricular activities all the time and not paying any attention at all to your studies. Now I've had it with you. I expect you to drop all your activities and get to work. And you can also stop all that blather about going to university next year. If you're lucky, and I repeat, if you're lucky, you can go to Teachers College next year, but you'd better pull up your socks and get to work. I can tell you right now you can say good-bye to your high-flying ideas about university."

I am astounded. Mrs. Kruk has spent hours with me over the past two years, talking with me, helping me to understand my life and behavior, and I thought she had done it willingly. Her guidance and support have helped me to keep my resolve not to steal, and to sort through the difficult times I always had relating with my fellow students and my family. And I thought I was doing fairly well in my courses. Just a month ago, during fall convocation, I had received the outstanding achievement award for grade eleven English. And now I learn that all my teachers hate me—or at least that is how I interpret my mother's version of that parents' night.

Confused and hurt, I quit every one of my extracurricular activities and speak to no one. I hate walking the halls, hate seeing my fellow students chat amicably with their teachers, hate every teacher of mine, and especially Mrs. Kruk for betraying me. The black rage, less frequent now, but a dammed-up force always ready to burst free, wells up inside me. Mrs. Kruk smiles at me in the hall but I turn away. It is a bad three weeks, at home and at school, and I learn nothing and accomplish nothing. Mr. Dow, my English teacher, comments on an assignment about where to construct the replacement for the old Jubilee Bridge, "Do you have any particular reason for writing like a twelve-year-old, or are you just trying to make a statement now that all your extracurricular activities have been curtailed?" and then jolts me with a grade of 49 percent on my fall report card. The grade, intended primarily to jump-start me, is justified; my mind is not on my studies. Why bother, I think, if I can't go to university. Finally, Mrs. Kruk corners me and demands to know what is going on.

I tell her, and she is aghast. "I did not say anything of the kind, and I'm sure your other teachers didn't either, but I'll check this out for you. You come to see me at four o'clock, promise!" It is a command, not a request. In response to my doubtful furrowed brow, she beams the full, warm smile that brought me around to trusting her in the first place. We meet, and talk, and try to find reasons for Mom's interpretation of what has been said. Evidently, Mom didn't want to talk about me at all during the conferences. She is still angry at the Glenlawn teachers for not getting

Billy through grade twelve. And then Mrs. Kruk says a curious and confusing thing, a remark that makes me furious with Mom at the time but many years later helps me to understand her motives with considerably more sympathy. "Sharon," she sighs, "your life would be a whole lot easier if you weren't so bright."

Bright? My grades plummet in every subject after that episode; I come within a hair's breadth of not qualifying for university admission even if it were offered; and I begin to question whether I am actually capable of succeeding at university.

NOVEMBER 10, 1964. "WHAT IS THIS GARBAGE I HAVE FOUND in your pockets?" At age twenty, I am still living with my mother during my second year of teaching, but hope, wrongly as it turns out, that I am no longer subject to her periodic checks of my pockets. "What kind of young woman has this in her pockets? Trash! You're nothing but cheap trash!" With that, she contemptuously flushes the prophylactic suppositories I use for birth control down the toilet.

Later that evening, as I walk from the bus stop to my boyfriend's boardinghouse, I stop at a drugstore to buy replacements as well as some Contac C for a cold that is just starting. Unfortunately, rehearsals for a community production of *All's Well That Ends Well*, in which I play Diana, have exhausted my spending reserves with extra bus fare and snack money, and I discover that I have to choose between Contac C and my birth control. Between full-time teaching a grade six class sixteen miles north of St. Vital and my role in the play, opening the following week, I know I can't get sick. I choose the Contac C. Then I visit Robert.

DECEMBER 15, 1964. "WELL, OF COURSE, WE'LL HAVE TO WAIT for the test results, but all my years of experience tell me that you are indeed pregnant," the doctor says. "I assume it's that young man who saved you from hypothermia up north last winter—just about a year ago next week, isn't it? That's okay then. If you got through that together, you'll be able to manage."

Something in my eyes must have caused Dr. Flett to doubt for a moment my ability to "manage," because he paused, then said, as though introducing a totally new topic of conversation, "Terrible situation at the hospital this morning. Young girl, little bit younger than you, brought in by her roommate, bled to death right in the emergency room. She'd decided to have a back-street abortion. Of course, I know you are smarter than to do something like that. Count on your fellow. He pulled you through last year. He'll pull you both through this."

Last year. Christmas of 1963. Robert's Volkswagen had skidded into a snowbank in the remote northern interlake region twenty miles from the nearest reservation, more than forty miles from the nearest town. As we struggled to push the car out of its white prison, we hoped that one of the eight cars on Jackhead Reservation, where Robert taught school, would pass by en route to the neighboring Peguis Reservation and rescue us. Seven hours later, exhausted from the cold that invaded every pore of my body, I relinquished myself to sleep, to a dream of a warm, cozy room with a roaring fireplace. I felt so good that I resisted Robert's persistent shaking until he threatened to slap me awake. Forced to open my eyes, I realized I was colder than I had ever been in my life, cold to the bone, colder than I had ever thought it possible to be. I fought to go back to my warm and comfortable dream, but Robert would not let me. Five hours after that—almost thirteen hours after we had slid off the road—we were rescued. Only after I checked out my still-throbbing toes and fingers with my doctor two days later did I learn that Robert had undoubtedly saved my life.

That alone was not a solid basis for a marriage but, in my inexperienced view, love was. Six weeks after my appointment with Dr. Flett, Robert and I were married on a Saturday afternoon, his mother came for Sunday dinner, and we both returned to teaching at our respective schools on Monday.

Six months later, on a balmy evening in June, two days before my twenty-first birthday and six weeks before our baby was due, I packed my suitcase and left our apartment. Robert watched and laughed, "You'll be back." My suitcase was heavy, containing the baby's layette and maternity and ordinary clothes for me. I had thirty-four dollars in my pocket, seventy-five dollars in the bank, and eighty extra pounds of toxemia-augmented baby fat. Literacy provided no salvation in this situation. I could not take any pleasure from reading, since all I seemed able to focus on in what I read were couples who loved each other and prospective fathers who were looking forward to their children. Similarly, I could not read anything about pregnancy, since all of that material also assumed loving couples and happy fathers. On the other hand, when eventually I did read *The Scarlet Letter*, I certainly understood what Hester Prynne was going through!

I walked awkwardly and clumsily toward the bus stop but couldn't decide which bus I wanted to take. I walked a few blocks west, and then a few blocks south, away from the downtown area and back into the residential area. With so little money, even one night in a hotel was more than I could afford. My mother was living less than five miles away, a few blocks from the school where Robert taught, but I couldn't go there. When I'd told her

I was pregnant, she had replied, "I'll tell you this once, and once only. When you leave this house, you don't come back to it. You made your bed; you lie in it." Only after I had my own child did I realize that parents say those things in the furor of the moment but rarely hold their children to them. But now I took her words at face value, recalling the time I had gone to her house for a visit and taken a short walk in the neighborhood to relieve my aching back. "How can you walk through this neighborhood like that?" she'd remonstrated. "People know that you are the wife of a teacher in the high school. You could damage his reputation in the community." So now I walked a few blocks east, and then a few blocks north, and ended up back at our tiny basement apartment, knocking on the door, feeling lonely, dejected, and humiliated. I put my unpacked suitcase under the bed, a silent reminder that I was not totally subjugated to this man I loved, who had fathered our child and agreed to marry me but who had not yet decided to love me.

"WOULD YOU LIKE TO GO TO UNIVERSITY?" ROBERT ASKS. IT IS May 1967, our son will be two years old in August, and I am teaching grade four at a school less than ten miles from home. Robert's mother is living with us in the living room of our two-bedroom apartment. Robert's question, coming at the end of a long day, astounds me. University has slowly receded from my list of immediate desires and goals.

"What? Yes. How? Why?" I ask.

"The Department of Education is soon going to require all teachers to have their B.A.'s. School boards will be letting go those teachers who don't upgrade their education. We might as well get started right now. I'll teach and do nights and summer school; you do days and summer school."

"DON'T COUNT ON HAVING AN HOUR HERE AND AN HOUR THERE to do your studying and homework," cautions Professor Clake, who in addition to being my adviser is also my psychology professor. "Organize your assignments and your studying in ten- and fifteen-minute bits of time, because with a small child that's all the time you'll have." That is the best advice I receive during my undergraduate education. My meager savings allow just enough for a half-day babysitter, Robert's mother, who lives with us but works in the afternoons, so I schedule all my classes in the mornings and study and keep house in the afternoons and evenings. With no office or desk space, and just the kitchen table, which needs to be cleared for dinner, to work on during David's nap time, I learn to take advantage of every minute. I also learn to divide tasks into manageable bits, such as sorting out my bibliography, or writing an opening sentence, or revising two pages, or summarizing five pages of a chapter, or memorizing a page of notes—all jobs that can be reasonably completed in ten or fifteen minutes. With such a system I can be organized and thorough, but I develop no idea of how to work and play with concepts, how to question assumptions, or how to relate what I am learning to my own life. My studies are compartmentalized into David's nap time and any stolen moments that unpredictably offer themselves, totally separate from my "real" life as a wife and mother. I read and analyze poems in Whitman's *Leaves of Grass* but do not observe, stroke, or rest my head and mind on a leaf of grass. I read and discuss the transcendental nature of Emerson's "transparent eyeball," with which we come to understand inner reality through external happenings, and external reality through our inner vision, but I cannot transcend the stasis of my domestic life. At one point, after losing myself to intellectual passion in a class discussion of civil disobedience in Thoreau, and then finding myself defending the authority of my husband's views over my own, I am confronted by my English professor, Marta Kruuner, who demands to know how I can hold such conflicting perspectives simultaneously. When I tell her I have to because I have vowed to honor my husband, and therefore to honor his views, she responds with deliberate overstatement, "Then you'd better get rid of that husband!"

I am aghast. "But I love him."

"Just because you love him, you don't need to love all his ideas, and you don't need to consider your ideas inferior to his. You've shown today, in your discussion of Emersonian transcendentalism, what a fine mind you have. You need to learn to value your own thoughts, even if they are different from your husband's. Otherwise, you will never know what you are fully capable of achieving."

IT WAS A DISTURBING CHALLENGE. THE SUPERIORITY OF HUS-bands, fathers, and older brothers was unquestioned in my world, and now a professor whom I esteemed very highly was challenging this notion, telling me that my ideas and opinions were as valid as my husband's. A tiny crack appeared in the fragile eggshell of my perspective of what is appropriate in a marital relationship, a crack that would eventually break open and destroy that enclosure, releasing a creature free to discover her place in a world suddenly widened beyond previously proscribed boundaries.

One of those boundaries is the line between truth and perception. Truth is presented to us while we are still very young as some sort of absolute value. It exists, we are led to believe, in some kind of pure, unalterable state, impressive most of all in its unadulterated singularity. People who tell "the truth" and who uphold "the truth" are good people; those who don't, aren't. As we discover that our perception differs from the perceptions of others, we come into conflict sorting out who is right, because if truth is absolute, only one version of an event or an idea can be right. On the other hand, if only one version of an event or idea can be right or true, how do we account for credible individual perceptions? Might differing perceptions be valid as a kind of personal truth? But if truth can be personal, then how can it be absolute? These are questions that I did not articulate explicitly but pondered in a muddled kind of way all the while I was growing up.

William Faulkner and Henry VIII helped me to clarify the muddle.

Writing about Faulkner's narrators in *Absalom, Absalom!* provided my first explicit literacy experience with multiple truths. In that novel, four narrators take turns telling the same story, each genuinely unaware of the motivations, biases, and personal history that have shaped and inevitably distorted his or her idiosyncratic selection and interpretation of events. Each version is compellingly different. Faulkner uses the image of a pebble tossed into a pond, causing ripples to the edge of the pond and corresponding invisible countercurrents, to represent the vast and varied implications of any single event. That tossed pebble image forces the question: Can one person, alone, offer a true version of any event, even when everything said by that person is true?

Thinking and writing about this was not an enterprise to fit into ten or fifteen minutes of free time. It demanded a reconceptualization of everything I had considered to be reality. It taught me to understand and respect the views of others that are different from my own. It taught me, also, to respect my own views within the context of alternative views.

Yet even powerful new ideas need buttressing. About two weeks after completing my essay on Faulkner's narrative structure, I heard two very different, mutually incompatible, lectures on Henry VIII in my British history class. Professor Batzel first presented Henry VIII as he is traditionally portrayed in history: a brilliant but self-absorbed tyrant, indulging in his lusts, using his wives' inability to bear him a son as a lever to overthrow the power of the Roman Catholic Church in his personally motivated desire for divorce and remarriage, and in his politically motivated desire for supreme authority. The second lecture showed us a Henry very different in motivation. In a time of national and international unrest, Henry needs a son to secure the right of succession. Forced by custom to wed the infertile widow of his deceased brother, Henry has no choice but to separate from the established church to gain a divorce so that he can marry someone who will bear him a son. Truly dismayed at each successive wife's lack of ability to produce a male heir, he reluctantly and with distress divorces or beheads them in order to secure his line of succession.

By the end of this lecture, although entirely aware of Dr. Batzel's intellectual manipulation of my emotions, I was nonetheless more ready to credit Henry VIII with sensitivity and humanity than I had been before. More important, I realized for the first time how problematic history is, how vulnerable to misrepresentation even when based on supposedly undisputed facts and evidence. And then I integrated the history lesson with the insights I had gained from Faulkner's book to understand just how arbitrary and subjective knowledge is, even though often presented as an unchallenged body of agreed-upon certainties.

Excited by this synthesis, I introduced it during dinner time conversation and was roundly rebuked by Robert for trying to show off before his mother and making her feel uncomfortable. Dr. Kruuner's comment about giving up my husband if that was the only way to realize my own potential flashed red behind my eyes, and I realized that in this home as well as in my growing-up home I needed to keep my evolving understanding to myself.

In the fall of 1969, I was teaching junior high English at a large secondary school five miles from my home. During fall convocation at the University of Winnipeg, I received my B.A. degree. The program listed me as one of two graduates who had been awarded a fellowship for master's work at the University of Manitoba, a generous award that would have given me free tuition plus $5,500 a year. However, our son was only in kindergarten and still required a part-time babysitter. Robert would reluctantly agree to my accepting the award only if I agreed to have his mother, who a year earlier had moved to her own apartment nearby, move in with us again.

I was torn. The opportunity to continue at the university was beyond any of my expectations. On the other hand, the prospect of again leaving all decisions about our son's upbringing to Robert's mother and of losing the living room of our two-bedroom apartment to provide a bedroom for her was too overwhelming. Robert had gambled on my love for learning as a way to bring his mother back into our home. He was truly shocked when I decided instead to return to teaching. I declined the fellowship and accepted a position at Churchill High School. The decade of the sixties was over.

6

Evil Woman? Bad Mother? Single Parent!

ESCAPING THE EPITHETS

Would it have been worth while,

To have bitten off the matter with a smile,

To have squeezed the universe into a ball

To roll it toward some overwhelming question,

To say: "...

... I shall tell you all"—

If one ...

   Should say: "That is not what I meant at all.

   That is not it, at all."

—T. S. Eliot: *"The Love Song
of J. Alfred Prufrock"*

One inescapable feature of the literacy narrative is that it requires the writer to discover connections and determine reasons for what now *seems* to have happened in the past. Such invention is unavoidable, but also begs the question, To what extent can these connections and reasons be "true"? If fiction requires of its readers the willing suspension of disbelief, what does a literacy narrative require? In response to that question, I

offer an invitation to allow "the cool web of language," as Robert
Graves calls it, to wind you in, to bring you into a verisimilitude
that is my own creation, and my perception and understanding
of my own truth, at this moment.

ROBERT IS SPEAKING AND THE SITUATION IS HEARTBREAKING.
"You realize, don't you, that your life will never be as good as it is now. If
you break up this marriage to live with her, you will not be able to keep
your job as a teacher. Moral turpitude, they will call it, and they will use
that to force you out. You're making a big mistake."

It is 1976, and my marriage of eleven years is breaking up. I am
regretfully aware of living out the predictions of my freshman psychology
textbook, from which I learned that adults who have difficult childhoods,
adults from different cultures, and adults who marry young all have higher
divorce rates than more mature adults from similar cultures and with less
troubled childhoods. There is a dilemma in advanced literacy. The more we
read about how individuals in similar situations have coped (or not coped),
the more our expectations are shaped—expanded or constrained—for ourselves and for others. Statistics can be particularly seductive with the allure
of empirically quantifiable evidence. It can become too easy to decide that
since most people in a particular category don't make it, it is unlikely that
I—or some other person—will make it. There is a danger in not paying
sufficient attention to the rugged resilience of the human spirit.

What my undergraduate education seems to have taught me, in part,
is that my premature pregnancy and marital breakup are predictable, almost
inevitable, consequences of my early childhood. I want to reject that hypothesis; I want to be in charge of my life, not living a life preordained by forces
beyond my control. As though to spite the predictions, I have stayed married
for eleven years to a man who will not say that he loves me or needs me,
but whose religion and culture and own sense of values require him to take
responsibility for the child he has fathered.

From the start, our marriage was plagued by our different responses
to my pregnancy. His first words, "What will I tell my mother?" signaled
the heavy burden of culturally induced and maternally induced guilt he
carried. He seemed to feel that to be happy with me would be an insult to
the standards exacted by his Mennonite community, particularly by his
mother, whereas I had a simpler, more primitive view that a child conceived
in love and brought up in the comfort of that love should bring dishonor
to no one. One event encapsulates the cultural burden of guilt that infected
our happiness. While driving through Altona to visit his mother soon after

David's birth, Robert demanded, in his unhappy shame, that I hold our baby underneath the dashboard as we wove our way through the streets of the small town. To my own unhappy shame, I complied.

My continued compliance and obvious devotion caused Robert to remark at the breakup of our marriage, "I thought your love was so strong that I could say anything, do anything, and you would still be constant with your feelings toward me." I had thought so too, but life proved us both wrong.

The first serious indication of trouble came almost two years before the breakup during a drama-in-education class. The dozen or so members of the class had been exploring theatrical possibilities in music, dance, and games by moving in tempo to an eighteenth-century composition that ranged from quiet serenity to passionate turbulence, all the while tossing a colorful ball, about eight inches in diameter, to others in the group. Irresistibly drawn in by the pulse of the music, I began to dance and to toss the ball in throws ranging from easy lobs to hard, straight hurls. My motions caught the instructor's eye, and he leaped into the center of the group, catching the ball, whirling round, and then pitching it to me in an elegant arc. I returned in kind, and within moments the others in the class became a circle around the two of us lobbing, tossing, pitching, hurling, flinging, and heaving, all the while matching our rhythms and mood to the passionate rise and fall of the music. At the break, he asked for a sip of my Coke, took the bottle, and guzzled deeply without first wiping the edge, as was the custom when sharing a pop. Our eyes caught and held, and I knew that the turbulence I was feeling was not what I ought to be feeling.

Had I been older or more mature—or, possibly, more widely read— I might have relished the moment as an exquisite peak of high energy and excitement, sexual only in potential, not in occurrence. As it was, denied overt affection at home, I saw it as a threat to my marriage and worried about it for days. I became conscious of being drawn to men who used the same scent of aftershave my husband used, and of being excited by the rough tweed of a man's jacket. An innocent compliment became an enticement, an appreciative glance an invitation to dalliance. I seemed to be sinking into a sea of lurid possibilities, and I was both excited and terrified. I decided that my best defense would be to avoid all opportunities to be alone with men. I felt resentful that Robert refused to accompany me to staff parties, the theater, and other outings, so that I had to build this defense, but nonetheless I was satisfied I had chosen the best way to avoid temptation.

At home, as Robert would slightly flinch in response to my nightly kiss, eager for me to be off to bed so that he could enjoy his solitude and his beer, I spoke my concerns. But he had his own world of difficulties that he could not or would not share with me, and neither of us could escape our individual troubles long enough to appreciate each other's. This is not to say that we had a completely unsatisfying life together. Had I been content to live a life of near-solitude, visiting and being visited by only close relatives, and had I been willing to take for granted his unspoken need for a secure family life, and had I been content to define my existence within the parameters of his existence, our marriage could probably have survived. But I was not content.

Not wanting to cut myself off from all social interaction, I began to take piano lessons again, and to study music history, in addition to taking modern jazz dancing lessons with a neighbor who welcomed a weekly break from her four small children. Not everything was "beautiful at the ballet," however. I was escaping rather than confronting my domestic problems, and I couldn't figure out a next step when I was receiving no response to my first step. It might have seemed natural to find some solace or guidance through literacy, through self-help books or books on the sociology of the family, or even an escape into romantic fantasy, to live a vicarious life of passion, but literacy has rarely played those roles in my life. I read for pleasure, for intellectual, professional, and emotional growth, and for information but seldom have found satisfaction in reading for explicit personal guidance or total escape.

Instead, I developed a close companionship with a woman who shared my love of music and theater. Together we attended concerts and plays, spending hours afterward discussing our responses to them. Both in our late twenties, we were like teenagers exchanging stories of our lives and loves. I was fascinated by the freedom she had experienced in the major romantic interludes of her life, and we began increasingly to share intimate details of our respective relationships with men. Her spicier seasoning of experience excited me, and her stories made me wonder about the more exotic aspects of sex. It must have been a gradual set of circumstances that altered our relationship, but the actual happening was relatively sudden and unexpected. Robert had gone fishing for the weekend, and I had invited her over to spend the evening with David and me. All three of us had gone for a long walk, laughing and talking and having an unusually funny and boisterous time. When we returned, we all contributed to cooking a dinner, with continued laughter and kibitzing. David and I both appreciated this exuberant and rollicking change from our usual quiet and orderly existence. Finally exhausted, David went to bed, and she began to help me, as she often did, with my piano. She took pieces I had been working on for weeks—a Chopin polonaise, a Mozart sonata, and a Brahms ballade—and played them at sight, bringing to life and clarity melodies and harmonies that were muddied and chaotic in my playing. I was mesmerized by the strength, agility, and sensitivity of her fingers as the piano responded to her touch with depth and resonance. Then we opened a bottle of wine, lit some candles, and began to talk, long into the night. At some time, I suggested that she take off her shoes, which for some reason she was reluctant to do. As I took off mine, I understood her hesitation. Shoes have a way of defining distance; taking them off rendered us both more vulnerable. It seemed natural, as I grew increasingly tired, to rest my head in her lap as we talked, and for her to stroke my hair. Then, accidentally or not, she caressed my face, and I sat up suddenly. Neither of us spoke, but we both knew we were at some kind of watershed.

Being with her was like being in a capsule of warm sunlight. I felt loved, protected, appreciated, pampered, and needed for the first time in my life. At the same time, I realized that I had fallen into the very trap of deceit that I had been trying to avoid. By avoiding situations that might lead to infidelity with a man, I had become unfaithful to my husband with a woman. I talked incessantly about her with Robert and his immediate family, as though subconsciously trying to raise alarms in their minds so they could help me resolve the situation, but I could find no way to bring the affair either into the open or to an end.

Eventually, I simply told the truth and ended my marriage. The legal system shunned me, my lawyer not even wanting to handle the case after I told him the circumstances of the breakup. My husband's lawyer came up with an unthwartable plan. Unless I agreed to it, Robert would sue for custody, would have a strong case because of my relationship with a woman, might win, and, in any event, would force a lengthy and expensive court battle that would hurt all of us. I could avoid this custody suit and court battle by signing away all rights to maintenance (which I considered just, since I was working full time) and all rights to child support (which I considered less just). Legally, it was brilliant. Ethically, I had my doubts, but I signed. At the time, seeing my behavior as my husband and my lawyer saw it, I accepted the familial and legal shunning as warranted.

And yet my life did not seem evil, and my mothering did not seem inappropriate. When David and I were having the usual parent-child difficulties that arise during adolescence, my friend would serve as a sympathetic intermediary, patiently listening to David and helping him to work out some of his frustrations. We were like catalysts spurring each other on to new and interesting projects. I learned how to refinish furniture, read a complete orchestral score, renovate an old bedroom, and have an orgasm. We worked together, played together, and traveled together as a caring family of two adults and a child. And, to my surprise and relief, we were accepted in both our professional and social communities as a caring family of two adults and a child.

Robert's predictions of professional rejection were not borne out. Within six months I was made chair of the English department in my school as well as of the divisionwide English curriculum committee. The change in my teaching was dramatic. Having gone into public school teaching reluctantly, I had viewed it only as a job, an important job requiring responsibility and dedication but still primarily a job. With the security of a husband, I had felt that if teaching did not work out, I could quit and retrain for something else or even have another child. Without a husband, I realized that teaching was no longer just a job; it was my career. Through night school and summer school, I completed my B.Ed. and began work on my master's, while rising through the executive positions of the Manitoba Association of Teachers of English to become its president. But those were just surface indicators of a much deeper change in my teaching.

As I had challenged rules in my youth, considering them designed to keep in line those who otherwise would not know how to behave, I had similarly eschewed teacher guides to readers and other textbooks, and had used curricula as general guides rather than as scripture carved in stone. Intuition told me that if children read a lot and wrote a lot, and enjoyed their reading and writing, and could talk about how their texts related to themselves as human beings in the world, they would want to learn. Wanting to learn, they would be ready to benefit from the scaffolding provided by rules of text generation (the grammar of process), textual form (the grammar of product), and critical analysis and interpretation (the grammar of response). In other words, they would want to understand language and structures of language in reference to their increasing desire to read and write with more confidence and competence, because they would see themselves as communicating to others and interacting with written text in meaningful, engaging ways. Unfortunately, I did not have the theoretical background to give me confidence in my intuitions and to argue their validity, and so I wavered almost schizophrenically between traditional expectations of what goes on in English classrooms and my own views of what should go on in English classrooms. When my intuitions were challenged, I succumbed to the traditional. For example, a couple of years after my marital breakup, I began the school year having my grade twelve class write something every day. Each night I quickly read what they had written, circling all the bits that struck me as excellent, promising, well-crafted, or insightful writing—a word with just the right nuance; a clear transition; a delightful image; a powerful metaphor. Each day I read one example from each person's paper, explaining why it was good and then, after the first week, asking the class to explain why each selection might have been chosen, with the intention of soon having them select good bits from each other's papers and explain why to the rest of the class. The students responded by writing with well-constructed images, clear transitions, parallel structures, delightful metaphors, and so on. They increasingly enjoyed writing, and I increasingly enjoyed reading their writing.

Then the demon of grades appeared. Continuous progress is often translated into continuous evaluation, and home room teachers began clamoring for the marks demanded by our school system of grading. Unfortunately, as soon as a grade is slapped on a piece of writing, some justification must be made, and even though I praised my students for imaginative risk taking, my justification for any grade below an A was embedded in what was "not right" in traditional terms of conventional academic prose. As I acquiesced to the pressure for grades, my students regressed to their wary, safe, typical school-like writing, and the creative impetus that sparked some of the best writing produced in my grade twelve classes flagged. Because I did not know enough to challenge the demand for weekly grades, which is quite distinct from continuous progress and assessment, I abandoned my intuitions and followed systemic expectations. However, even while temporarily abandoning my intuitions in the classroom, I made a commitment to learn how to develop and defend them. This professional commitment was something quite new, something that began to grow as my new independence showed me that I was an individual capable of taking charge of my life and shaping it according to what I valued. Even more important, I came to realize that those values, although not in the standard systemically prescribed straight line, were nonetheless valid.

This new confidence was nurtured by the emotional and intellectual support of my friend. A welcoming hug, a gentle touch, a stroke of the hair, a warm, accepting arm around the shoulder, a lap to rest the work-tired head: these were the foundation stones of our physical support for each other; these were the manifestations of affection that I had never before experienced, not in my childhood home and not in my marital home. And our physical support for each other was buttressed by long hours of talking, from the mundane trivia of workday problems and challenges to larger questions of education, art, music, literature, politics, and society. In that twenty-month period I felt I was moving through thirty years of life, catching up on all the hugging and holding and talk about my evolving understanding of the world that I had missed.

But the stronger I felt about myself as a teacher and as a person, the worse our relationship became. My friend seemed most content when I was dependent and needed her. Nor was the situation the best for my son, whose own mercurial moods were increasingly confounding the growing tensions in the home. I loved, respected, and admired her as a friend I could rely on, as a person I wanted to share ideas and experiences with but not the person to share my whole life with. It was as though, having caught up with all the physical cuddling and nurturing I had craved as a child, I was less needful, less desperately needful.

Breaking the relationship was a completely self-centered act. I had turned to her in need, and once that need was filled, I turned away. Disposable people. How could I do that to anyone, and particularly to one who had devoted almost two years to building a life with me. I could rationalize by describing our constant tension and frequent arguments in some kind of attempt to distribute blame and present myself more favorably. But the truth, as I saw it, was that I wanted to try life on my own. The irony was heavy; she had helped me feel good about myself; feeling good about myself precipitated my leaving.

But I knew I was hurting her, just as I knew by then that I had hurt Robert by leaving him. I wondered, What right do I have to hurt these people I have loved? What responsibility do I have for other people whose lives have become bound up with my life? What responsibility do I have to myself? What do I do if being responsible to who I am necessitates hurting someone else?

"OF COURSE, HE COMES FROM A SINGLE-PARENT FAMILY. WHAT can you expect?" I am in the staff room of the high school where I chair the English department, discussing with a colleague a grade twelve student whose grades have suddenly begun to fall dramatically and whose behavior has rapidly deteriorated. We are trying to determine the best way to help this young man recover sufficiently to graduate.

A single-parent family. My colleague's remark is well-intentioned and reasonable inasmuch as the student's parents have been divorced less than a year, and his mother is coping on a salary just above minimum wage. Nonetheless, her observation illustrates not only acknowledgment of and concern for the challenges facing single parents and their children but also an increasingly convenient label that is often erroneously posited as a cause or strong correlate of deviant or disruptive behavior.

My son lives in a single-parent family, even though he visits with his father at least once a week. Is he destined to live up to or down to societal expectations for children of single-parent families? I wonder how constant media characterizations of single-parent families as a major liability to the health, behavior, and general well being of today's young people actually contribute to shaping their behavior and influencing their attitude toward the world. How many single parents, usually women, are made to feel guilty for having left a disastrous or unsatisfactory marriage, only to find themselves labeled "single parent," trapped in the sticky web of correlation between that designation and the breakdown of societal mores? How many youngsters hear on the television, read in the headlines, and learn in their classrooms that to be a child in a single-parent family is to be out of the most socially desirable situation, to be part of a frequently cited explanation for or correlation between juvenile crime, juvenile depression, juvenile misbehavior, even juvenile suicide? How many thereby feel ineluctably led into and then trapped by disruptive and self-damaging behavior?

As a single parent from the time my son was ten years old, I am not raising these questions in a theoretical vacuum but rather within the emotional morass of guilt, confusion, and blame I undergo as my child negotiates the tricky path from adolescence to adulthood. Fortunately for both of us, literacy is his salvation as it has been mine. Introduced to books as soon as he could chew on them, he immersed himself thoroughly in the joys of reading and writing. By age seven he had written a seventy-two-page story of a lost Indian princess; by age eleven he had had his first poem published; by age fourteen he had outlined a one-hundred-and-thirty-seven-volume concept of a new comic series, with a superhero named Icon. Through all of the usual mother-son tensions, we shared this absorption with literacy.

AT THIS TIME OF WRITING, MY SON HAS JUST TURNED TWENTY-nine, has just had his first play, *The Reverend Otis Show*, produced on stage, and lives on his own in Winnipeg. Our shared penchant for written literacy does not extend to frequent letters, but we talk almost weekly over the telephone about our recent reading and writing. It is the bond that has overcome obstacles of growing up, of domestic discord, and of the dividing space of continents.

Obie, a sheltie puppy, now shares my home. I have watched him these past months learn how to behave in a home, how to be comfortable among strangers, and how to defend his territory from encroaching ducks, geese, cats, rabbits, chipmunks, and other dogs. The first time he encountered a goose, hissingly protective of her nearby brood, he stood transfixed, neither advancing nor retreating. It seemed as though he had calculated the risk of guarding his territory against the threat of the equally territorial goose almost twice his size, had rejected both options of retreat and attack, and had settled on a dignified neutrality. However, not wanting the many geese on the lake to seek sanctuary on my property, I had to figure out a way for him to discover that he did indeed have the right and the power to frighten the goose back into the water.

He stood curious and motionless, his ears up at the alert, one white-booted paw raised as though he were more pointer than sheltie. I moved toward the goose, stamping my feet heavily, urging Obie to "Chase that goose away!" The goose snaked her neck at me, hissing loudly as she thrust menacingly forward, looked uncertainly at Obie and furiously at me, and spread her wings. I hugged and praised Obie as though he had been entirely responsible. The next time geese invaded his territory, he walked calmly toward them, confidently moving them onto the lake. Thereafter, he quite firmly kept them off the grass, ignoring their hissing and their angrily writhing necks.

Watching this development of Obie's self-assurance, I felt simultaneously mother-proud and poignantly sad. Why could I not have responded as supportively to David's fear of arithmetic? Why could I not have built up his self-esteem in sporting activities? Why could I not have played his favorite game when I was tired after a day at work, just as I now chase Obie around the table at the end of the day? Why could I not have learned, not have discerned, when and why he needed a hug?

Part of the answer is that between teaching full time and taking courses at night school and summer school, I was too exhausted to provide the necessary support even had I been aware of what I should do and how I should do it. Part of the answer is that I was very young and completely ignorant of how to rear a child. But I think the most significant part of the answer is that the style of parenting modeled during my growing-up years did not focus on feelings and on the development of confidence and self-esteem. Almost as though to exemplify that idea, my son telephoned me two days after I had written the above sentence with another "delicious remark from Grandma Hamilton." They had been talking about my dog, Obie, and my mother had said to David, "I don't know why she didn't just get a little girl from the Children's Aid instead of a dog; it would require much less time and trouble." Quite simply—and with what a chilling feeling of guilt I realized this—my puppy was thriving under more patience and more understanding than I had ever learned how to give my son.

ANGRY AND HURT AFTER THE SEPARATION, ROBERT WAS UNWILL-ing to communicate with me and preferred to send messages through David: "I will pick David up on Sunday at 10:00. Please have him ready. Bob." Feeling culpable for the breakup, I acquiesced. Because he was the only line of communication between Robert and me, David found himself in a controlling role that enabled him to manipulate to the maximum. For example, when he was out with his father and it was time to come home, David pretended to telephone me and then told his dad I was not home. He kept this up until after midnight, even on a school night, hoping that his father would invite him to stay overnight, something Robert never did, even though he had unlimited visitation access. I was furious at Robert for keeping David out so late, and Robert was furious at me for not being home to receive David at a reasonable time on a school night. And David, who openly admits to not wanting Robert and me to get together again, was quick to learn how to orchestrate our emotions to that end.

It was, of course, too much responsibility to place on David. He quickly perceived Robert's need to remain angry with me, and he exaggerated, embellished, magnified, even made up events to serve that need. It took him longer to realize that I held no anger, only sorrow, and so recognized sooner the deceptions in the tales he carried from one to the other of us. Although willing to admit these falsifications years later, he refused to admit them at the time. In fact, David's major way of dealing with his world torn asunder by his parents was to envision his world the way he wanted it to be, manipulate it to get it that way, and if that didn't work, then energetically and blindly insist that it was, indeed that way. "Parents who are getting a divorce are supposed to be angry with each other," he asserted, laying for himself a rational foundation for the superstructure of exaggerated malice and deception that he erected, with our unacknowledged acquiescence, between his father and me.

Together, David and I maneuvered our lives among the triple burden of epithets that I allowed to invade my sense of self. I was an "evil woman" because I had left my marriage to live with another woman. That evil seemed exacerbated rather than lessened when, nearly two years later, that liaison also fell apart, demonstrating, it might seem, my inability to make a firm commitment to any human being. I was a "bad mother" because, in addition to working all day, I was attending university at night and in the summer to earn first my bachelor of education degree and then my master's degree, and therefore was not spending sufficient time with David. And I was a single parent, labeled daily in the media as a correlative factor in the breakdown of families and of social mores. It is a lot to be held accountable for!

I CLING TO IMAGES TO STEER ME THROUGH THE QUAGMIRE OF guilt that threatens continually to engulf me. They are treasures of the past that I take out of my memory to review when the present seems overwhelming. I linger over David's first Christmases, when his eyes grew big at the sight of colored lights, and he soaked in the sounds and smells of the festive season. I remember how through his joy and pleasure I developed new eyes and ears to experience my world. I feel in my memory how his whole little body throbbed with excitement and wonder, and that helps me to feel again, in the present, the ties of shared history that bind us together. Then another kinesthetic image takes over. I feel David, less than a year old, a heartbeat away, crying in empathy with my misery when Robert is out again with the fellows at the local pub. I almost relish his echo of my feeling but then realize my baby should be happy and smiling, not sad with my sadness. He thereby teaches me to put away my sobs and to laugh and sing so that my infant will share my happiness and not my sorrow. And that reminds me of his favorite childhood song, the one he would ask for night after night in the time we shared together just before he fell asleep:

> With a lurch and a bump and the rattle of a chain
> The old farm horse pulls the wagon up the lane
> With a load of fine turnips, all yellow and big
> For the brown-eyed cow, and the little pink pig.
> For now comes the winter when we all sit by the fire
> And the pig's in the sty and the cow's in the byre
> And there's no sweet grass when the hoar frosts start,
> So they're bringing up the turnips in the old farm cart.

It reminds me that seventeen years later he and I are still lurching and bumping along an uphill road and that, as mother and son, we are still inexorably a heartbeat away from each other.

7

You Judge a System by Those It Fails

Being literate, like all other aspects of social life, is remade and reconceptualized in new settings. What seems to stay the same is that the literate have definite advantages over the nonliterate, which as a result give them more power and influence, a greater range of choice in their lifestyle, what they think about, or do, or how they re-create themselves in what they enjoy.

—M. Meek, *On Being Literate,* 208

Of course, the greater the choice, the more decisions and the more counting of cost of these decisions, in human as well as economic terms. In this chapter I receive an astounding invitation to study for a doctorate at London University. Advanced literacy has opened this door, baring a threshold of decision making. Each decision involves human cost to others, most particularly to my son, as well as the usual economic and emotional cost. I have the opportunity to re-create myself, to change the direction of my life, to achieve, finally, at fortysomething, the goal I had as an eight-year-old. This chapter begins my journey of coming to understand the concept of advancing the literacy of my students while concurrently coming to understand the implications of advancing literacy in my own life.

"IT'S OKAY, MOM," DAVID SAYS. "I UNDERSTAND. I KNOW THAT this has been a hard year for you. I know that this is a chance for you to start all over again. I know how important it is, and so I understand why you become frustrated and angry when everyone seems to be setting up barriers. I didn't mean to upset you. It's okay."

It is May 1983, and David and I are sitting side by side in the bedroom that he will have to move out of when I leave for London the following month. He is seventeen years old and, like me, loves our Wellington Crescent apartment sixteen stories above the meandering Assiniboine River. By going to London for three years, I am turning his life upside down, again. Ten minutes earlier, something he said or did provoked me to a rage, and I lashed out verbally and physically, assailing him with angry epithets and his pillow with angry fists, before slamming myself out of his room. It is as though the black has returned, and I have reverted to the foul-mouthed imprecations and violent temper of my youth. What's more, this is not the first instance in recent months. This final year of preparing to leave for London to earn a Ph.D. has taken its toll on my emotional as well as my financial resources.

Regretful even before the slammed door has stopped resonating, I knock and meekly reenter. Just as David, my infant in arms, acknowledged my tears of sadness and joined me sobbing in empathy, so David, my teenager, acknowledges my frustration and reaches out in support. "Who's the adult here anyway?" I manage to laugh through my curtain of contrition.

The decision to go to London had been negotiated between us three years earlier. As the incoming president of the Manitoba Association of Teachers of English, I was automatically an affiliate representative on the executive board of the Canadian Council of Teachers of English, who were meeting in Vancouver in May 1980 for their annual convention. However, as the newest member of the executive, with no established or vested interests, I was the most dispensable. I was therefore assigned to show downtown Vancouver to two keynote speakers from Britain, who had arrived three days early for the conference. Not yet cognizant of their status in our profession—Harold Rosen, professor and chair of the department of English and media studies at London University, was a central figure in the international language-across-the-curriculum movement, and James Britton, professor emeritus of Goldsmith College of London University, was an educational theorist who had influenced English language teaching around the world—I shepherded them onto a local bus, and we set out together from the campus of the University of British Columbia to discover downtown Vancouver.

That bus ride was the first jolt to my traditional understanding of the relationship between language and learning. Within seconds, an infant of about a year and a half bawled loudly until her mother gently massaged the back of her head. Moments later, she shrieked with joy as she noticed another infant, a little boy, sitting right behind her. Then she began to look all around, punctuating each visual discovery with loud exclamations, all of them ear-splitting interruptions to the conversation I was trying to have with Harold Rosen and James Britton. A lifetime of having been silenced in public (whenever that was possible) and years of trying to subdue my own son's exuberant vocal displays in public had left me unprepared for and completely uncomprehending of Harold's reaction: "She sure knows how to use language to make a point, doesn't she?"

Language? This shrieking and bellowing was language?

Harold continued, "Listen to how she changes just slightly when she sees something new. Listen now. She's gone back to looking at that little boy. Hear the sounds change? She's responding to her world, and she's sharing her response with her mother." I listened, astounded, and heard changes in her shrieks and bellows that somehow did seem to correspond with whatever was catching her attention at the time. I began to wonder what kind of difference it would make if her mother, who was quiet, neither scolding nor encouraging, responded to her noises with supportive conversation. Would that nurture her development of language? What if she constantly scolded the infant for making noise? Might that inhibit her development of language? And then another loud clatter broke my chain of thought.

Five boys, about thirteen years old, bounded to the back of the bus, which by now was so crowded that one of them, still yelling to his comrades, took a seat beside James Britton. Whereas I would have scrunched defensively into a small space by the window, James seemed to expand into the loudly bantering boy's consciousness. "Are you off to school?" he began.

"Sure," replied the boy, while his buddies stopped to listen. Within seconds, each boy was participating in the conversation, laughing and joking with Harold and James, and by the time the bus stopped at their school, they seemed almost reluctant to leave the two gentlemen from England who had briefly entered their lives. Again, I was astounded. Through language, within moments, connections had been made that transcended generational and national boundaries.

I spent the week of that conference attending more acutely than ever before to what teachers, researchers, and educational theorists had to say about language and learning. In particular, I attended the keynote addresses and workshops given by my new friends from England, and the door to a whole new world of understanding language, literature, and learning opened up for me. At a three-day writing workshop conducted by James Britton, I learned how to encourage classroom writing that allowed children to explore events and ideas that were important to them. I learned ways to respond to writing to help children express their ideas more excitingly and effectively, and discovered that relationships between writing and experience were much more complex and interesting than the traditional focus on form and structure portrayed them to be. But Harold Rosen's closing address ignited the most explosive idea that I took away from that conference. Witty, articulate, and urbane, he lambasted the educational system by which he had gained this linguistic and rhetorical prowess. He decried it as elitist, classist, racist, and sexist. When I asked him how he could denounce the system that had educated him so well, he withered me with a look of dismay at my naïveté. "You never judge a system by those who succeed in it. Those people will likely succeed in any system. You judge it by those it fails."

Visions of previously invisible students rushed into my head. Invisible, I mean, with respect to honors, accolades, or even much attention during my school years. I remembered vaguely Room Eighteen at Norberry School, overflowing with ninth graders taking neither Latin nor French, mostly boys, and how we scrupulously avoided having anything to do with them, as though they were somehow tainted by their academic streaming. I had always thought that students in classes like Room Eighteen had failed in the system. It had never occurred to me that perhaps the system had failed them.

I turned to my own teaching, recalling the group of brilliant young writers and thinkers who I had wished could be put into a special honors class. I thought of the more mundane and basic kinds of grammar-based language activities I did with my non-university-bound classes. And the realization struck me that I was perpetuating an elitist system of education that was setting up a large number of students for failure. Harold scrutinized my reactions and then invited me to join him and James Britton for lunch. We talked about the ideas that had challenged my views of teaching and learning all week. Then, as they were about to leave for England and I for Winnipeg, Harold asked me if I had ever thought of doing a Ph.D.

"A Ph.D.!" I responded. "I've just begun my master's, and I'm scared stiff. I've found out at this conference just how little I know about teaching and learning."

James continued on from Harold, "You really should consider doing a doctorate."

Harold took over: "And you should do it at the London Institute. Here's my address at the Institute. Give me yours. I'll send you the information."

I flew back to Winnipeg higher than the stated Air Canada altitude of 33,000 feet. A Ph.D.! From London University! I could hardly believe it.

Then pragmatics burst the bubble of excitement. I had a fifteen-year-old son who was already dismayed at my taking course after course after course. I had only a couple of thousand dollars of savings. I had an excellent job as chair of the English department at J. H. Bruns Collegiate, with students that were a charm to teach. And I had just begun my Master of Education degree and would need four more courses to complete it.

David and I negotiated the following deal. He would continue at St. John's Ravenscourt, a private school that provided him partial scholarship to help with his tuition, until he graduated in three years. I would continue with my job while completing my master's. Meanwhile, I would save every penny I could over the next three years so that I would have enough not only for my tuition and living expenses in London but also for David's first year of university tuition, books, and residence at the University of Winnipeg. He would work part time during that first year of university and during the summer months, and then would share the cost of subsequent years of university with his father. It was a plan that required me to save almost thirty thousand dollars in three years. The toll was emotional as well as financial. Watching every penny was not so difficult, since I could keep my goal as something to hold onto. However, teaching English full time, including directing a major musical production each year, rushing to complete my master's, coping with the growing pains of a teenager, and completing all the necessary paperwork to move to another country for three years left me with no time to think through the implications of what I was doing. Not until the last two months of the 1983 school year did I realize that at thirty-nine years of age I would be jobless and homeless, an expatriate on an intellectual venture that might well be beyond my grasp. That fear made me jumpy and grumpy, and I think that was mostly what accounted for my frequent outbreaks of frustration like the one that began this chapter.

The week following my outburst, still in May 1983, two momentous things happened. The first was a two-page spread in the *Winnipeg Free Press* about a thirty-three-year-old man called Colin Fleming. It told how he had not been allowed to go home with his mother following his birth because she had been declared mentally and emotionally unfit to look after her children. However, the Children's Aid Society had also not allowed him to be adopted by his alleged birth father, a pilot in the Royal Canadian Air Force. The reason had been flimsy, bearing on the possible genetic inheritance of mental instability from his birth mother, Irene Fleming. At the time, I did not know that my mother's name was Irene Fleming. All I knew was that I had been born Karen Fleming and that I had a sister, Jackie Fleming.

Although I was formally introduced by my adoptive mother to Jackie, my sister, when I was eighteen, we had actually met, by accident and unknow-

ing of our sisterhood, when I was five and Jackie almost seven. My adoptive
mother and I were walking hand in hand downtown when she met an
acquaintance from nearby Transcona whom she had not seen for a couple
of years. The woman also had a little girl in tow, much too old for her to
have borne since she and Mom had last met, and the resemblance between
us, despite Jackie's bright red hair and more cheerful disposition, was remark-
able. The two women compared stories and discovered that Jackie, now
Jackie Rosskopf, had formerly been Jackie Fleming, with a sister thirteen
months younger called Karen. Wanting not to cause the two little girls any
more discomfort than they had already been through, our mothers decided
not to tell us until we were older.

One day, thirteen years later, Mom drove me to a small café on
Transcona's main street, parked the car, and went inside. She came out with
a young woman whom she introduced as "Jackie Rosskopf, your sister."
She then went back into the café, leaving us in the car to talk.

"But you were blonde. I remember you with blonde, curly hair," were
Jackie's first incredulous words.

"I was blonde until I was about four or five," I replied, remembering
some pictures Mom had taken shortly after she adopted me. "But how do
you remember me? I don't remember you at all."

"Well, you were just a baby when we were taken away from the
Flemings," she replied. "But I was already almost two years old, and I still
faintly remember crying and crying when they separated us. And I remember
playing with you because, when I went to the Rosskopfs soon after we were
separated, there was no one to play with."

And so we talked, nervously and self-consciously, two (un)related
beings whose lives had been intertwined for eight months eighteen years
earlier. Mostly what I felt was relief that this woman of twenty who was my
sister was pretty and friendly, and obviously a very nice, happy person. I
wanted to feel more; I felt I ought to want to hug her and to urge us to
become part of each other's lives, and I felt very guilty because I couldn't
find those emotions anywhere inside of me.

After about fifteen minutes, Mom rejoined us, Jackie had to leave for
an appointment, and the meeting was over. I felt inadequate on all counts.
I was not the little blonde baby she remembered, and I couldn't feel what
all the newspaper accounts of parted siblings meeting years later proclaimed
that I should feel. Her warm good humor and generous spirit made me feel
hopeful that our shared gene pool might eventually manifest itself in some
form of goodness in me, but I did not leap to any insights of kinship, and
I felt there was something wrong with me because of that.

And now, twenty years later, I saw what seemed to be a familiar pair of eyes staring at me out of the paper. A young man named Colin Fleming, with pointed chin and prominent jaw (like Jackie's and mine), is furious at the Children's Aid Society's treatment of him, the story said. Declared borderline autistic, Colin had not been allowed to be adopted by his own birth father but had been shuffled from foster home to foster home, brutally burned by cigarettes in one home and cruelly raped in another. Familiar echoes resounded, and I burrowed more deeply into the article. Evidently, Colin had several brothers and sisters, most of whom had been located by the time the story went to press. I thought about the limited information I had: Jackie Fleming, now age 40; Karen Fleming, age almost 39, and Colin Fleming, age 33, with several siblings. Might I be one of them?

It took me five days to make the call. I felt curious but detached, as though even if Colin were my brother, his existence still would not influence my life. The next day I would be flying to Montreal for a conference, and in a month I would be leaving my home and my son to live in London for three years. I was finishing off a school year and had a career as a secondary English teacher. I was incapable of coping with any more emotional stress. When I finally did call the *Winnipeg Free Press*, asking to speak to the reporter who wrote the story because I might be one of the siblings yet to be located, I was told that all the siblings had been found. The coolness of the response made me snap back, "Well, if the name Karen Agnes Fleming ever comes up, I'm her." I hung up too quickly for her to reply and was unaware of the furor my call caused in the newsroom or of next day's notice in the *Winnipeg Free Press* asking me to call back. The follow-up to that event would be put on hold until I returned from London three years later.

The second momentous occurrence of that week was the arrival of a slim envelope from the Social Sciences and Humanities Council of Canada awarding me a grant of almost eleven thousand dollars for the first year of my doctoral studies in England, with the potential for renewal each year of my stay in London if my research proved productive.

At the Montreal conference, Harold Rosen, who was the opening keynote speaker, informed me that he would be my tutor at the London Institute of Education. He suggested that, in preparation, I read Proust's *Remembrance of Things Past*. Entering the amazing and unfamiliar world of this late-nineteenth-century French aristocrat, I rediscovered my own world with new eyes. My attention was focused on how one simple event, such as walking up a flight of stairs, encompassed ten pages, while years might be skimmed over in a paragraph. Events that happened once might appear a half dozen times in different contexts for different reasons, while events that occurred many times might receive one brief mention. I came to appreciate how we do that with our lives constantly, reliving certain events over and over again, blocking out whole months, sometimes whole years, of our lives, and playing in slow motion events that to others may seem inconsequential but to us have portentous meaning (though we might not consciously know what that meaning is).

At over one thousand pages, *Remembrance of Things Past* is not a quick read, and I lived in this multifaceted world of Proust and the consequent rethinking of my own life for over a month. I became aware that Proust, as author of the story of his life, was equally author of his life; that in choosing which events to foreground or forget, he was not only making a literary artifact, he was constructing his life. It was not a long jump from that to the realization that I must also be author of my life, and that in choosing which of my memories I wished to foreground and which to forget I was shaping not only my past but also my present and potentially my future.

One particularly compelling notion in *Remembrance* is Proust's description of the psychological makeup of a human being as the sum total of everyone's reactions to him or her. This is a concept to pause over. I think of my earliest memories of people's reactions to me in my foster homes and at the Greenhouse, and one word predominates: *bad*. My mother would try to bolster my self-esteem in ways that made little sense to me: "Of course you're not ugly. Wash your face, comb your hair, and smile, and you'll be as pretty as any other little girl with a clean, smiling face," balanced always with the reminder, "Nobody's got time for feelings. Get rid of those feelings. Be like Topsy. Topsy just grew." My social memories are a disaster: my classmates had hurled *buckteeth* and *cooties* at me throughout my elementary and junior high years. Very few of the boys in high school found me sufficiently attractive to date. Less than a week into our marriage my husband announced that he had married me only because his mother had told him it was the right thing to do. In no one's eyes was I more particularly special than anyone else. Perhaps it is not necessary to feel special, but it seemed to me that everyone I knew was special to at least one other person, a mother, a father, a best friend, a spouse. My generous fellowship for study in England did not even impress my family. My mother hadn't told anyone about it because she "was afraid they had made a mistake and had given it to the wrong person."

If we are the sum total of others' reactions to us, there is no doubt that I was a loser. If Proust was right, why had I not just collapsed under the weight of these excoriations? Raising that question forced me to ask some harder questions and make connections. Probably the most important occurred when I overheard David, just days before I was to leave for England, complaining to a friend over the telephone that he was unloved and unwanted by his parents. I couldn't believe what I was hearing. Since the day he was born, I had vowed I would do all I could to prevent his ever feeling those same pangs of parental rejection that had soured my own childhood. After hearing his comment, I tried to reassure him that both his mother and his father loved him very much. I explained that I had done the very best I knew how to do under the circumstances. And as that thought was voiced, I suddenly realized that, of course, that's what my parents had done. I could recall no acts of unwarranted (in their minds) meanness, and many acts of kindness. It was not in either of them to hug and to praise and to express open affection to me, so how could I expect them to? All that was in them to do to make my life better than it had been, they had done.

That realization, while not denying or eradicating the conditions that caused me to feel wretched and unloved during most of my growing-up years, enabled me to acknowledge the good intentions and otherwise unlikely opportunities that they extended to me. They had given all that their personalities and awareness allowed them to give. What more could anyone ask than that?

That insight wiped away so much of the dark jealousy and anger that had blighted my spirit that I was able to make the next leap. People react to other people the way they do for a reason. My own behavior must have been a direct cause of the taunts and torments and rejection I had lived through. I had to fortify myself to deal with that one; it was so much easier to blame others for their insensitivity and cruelty or to label myself a complete loser. If who we are is determined by what we do and say, then it is my responsibility to bridge the huge gap between how I present myself and how I want others to perceive me. In other words, I need to figure out who I want to be and begin behaving the way I want to be. Then, without even worrying about how others will react, I will eventually become the kind of person I aspire to become.

And then the flaw in my reasoning hit me. I had looped a tautological circle that brought me right back to the days of trying to be Anne of Green Gables. But even though my conclusion at age thirty-nine was in many ways the same as my conclusion at thirteen, I understood it better. I saw that the only person's attitude I can change is my own and that I can choose how I will react to every event of every day. I can also choose how I will react to memories of past events. Like my new understanding that my adoptive parents had truly done the best they knew how, this Proustian-inspired new understanding of my ability to choose my attitude liberated me, as no previous understanding had, from the sludge of resentment.

It was at this time that I began to reconstruct my views of what literacy is all about. I had initially construed literacy in its narrowest forms of basic reading and writing, and had then broadened my definition to encompass the kinds of intellectual endeavor that I had encountered in my undergraduate education at the university. But my decades of struggle with the fundamental concept of how we become who we are made me realize that literacy is far more complicated than I had understood it to be.

Literacy at the basic level of reading and writing is, as the cliché has it, essential but insufficient. Just being able to read and write about other worlds and other visions will not help to achieve them. Literacy at the functional level of getting along in society may be deemed by some as sufficient, but it is not liberating or empowering. Getting by is not reaching for the stars. Literacy is not just knowledge; it is knowledge that transforms. I began to see how, in wanting to be like Anne of Green Gables, I had really wanted to be a better person, not Anne but a better me. And I thought of the Stephen Spender poem, "An Elementary School Classroom in a Slum," wherein he says that unless the maps of the world that hang in the classroom become a realizable map to those other worlds, and unless the dusty, smudged windows become a means of access to those other worlds, the lessons will mean nothing to the lives of these children. The literacy taught in their schools will not have the power to transform their lives. That is the starting point of intellectual discovery that I take with me to London.

8

To London! To London!

(BUT NOT TO VISIT THE QUEEN)

The great divide in literacy is not between those who have learned to read and write and those who have not yet learned how to. It is between those who have discovered what kinds of literacy society values and how to demonstrate their competencies in ways that earn recognition.

—M. Meek, *On Being Literate,* 9

This statement captures the essence of the three-year study I embarked upon at the University of London Institute of Education, although I could not have articulated it so clearly or succinctly at the outset. In fact, prior to reading that statement, I would not have crystallized it in quite the same way even now. Only after encountering Margaret Meek's assertion did I focus on that notion as a central concept in my research. And that is how literacy works. It enables us to discover new meanings in and interpretations of what we already know and understand. Other formulations enrich meaning, because they resonate with the disparate histories of both the writer and the reader. I understood my work according to my own formulations; now I understand it even better because of someone else's formulations interacting with my own.

BRITAIN IS A LAND OF LITERACY HERITAGE. ITS LEGENDS AND history are almost as familiar to Canadian students of my generation as the history of our own country, its monarchy reminiscent of the candy floss pink commonwealth that spread across the maps of my childhood, its theater the undisputed best in the world. History, monarchy, and theater: that pretty well sums up my literacy-based exposure to Britain before I arrive in the summer of 1983, six weeks before the official start of the university term.

Leaving my trunk in London, for six weeks I tour England and Scotland by train and coach, free from familial and professional responsibilities for the first time in twenty years. I discover the fabulous rose fields of Aberdeen, acres of color whose blooms will grace mansions and cottages from John o'Groat's to Gretna Green. I wander lonely as a cloud—or rather alone, not lonely—over Helvellyn, where Wordsworth climbed and conceived his wonderful poems. I feed the swans of Avon, dance with the Morris dancers in Durham, walk the backs of Cambridge, rise with the sun over the magnificent spires of Oxford, clamber over the cliffs of King Arthur's Tintagel, and weep in the ruins of the old Coventry Cathedral.

Back in London, I take an unheated basement flat in Chelsea and treat myself to a matinee production of John Osborne's *A Patriot for Me*, starring Alan Bates. I write out several questions and comments, thinking I will drop the letter off at the theater next time I am near the Haymarket in the hope that Alan Bates might take time to respond. That evening I decide I will spend my first Saturday night in London wandering through the Piccadilly, Soho, Leicester Square area. I put the letter in my purse, since I might walk past the Haymarket, hail a taxi as a special treat, and find myself flying through the air.

Twilight and a drizzling rain must have prevented my seeing the car that hit me, because I am almost across the King's Road, my mouth already forming instructions for the taxi driver, when suddenly I am catapulted into the wet night. As in Proust's *Remembrance*, the events of a few seconds seem drawn out, suspended in time. My first thought is that I am going to die far away from home, and nobody will know how to inform my family. Then I hear my arm break, a faint but sharp crack, and see it flail in front of me, seemingly inches from my body. And then I land, and at that instant I realize that I will not die and that my arm is still attached though hanging strangely loosely. Somebody gathers up my new Harrods umbrella, navy with a now-scarred wooden duck's head, and my purse, both of which are lying with me in the puddles of the King's Road. The woman whose car hit me asks if there is anything she can do. My eyes fall on the letter to Alan Bates, poking unscathed out of my purse, and I try to mouth a reply. Nothing comes out but a husky rush of breath, and then I hear a faint raspy voice that seems to come from someone else, "Take this to Alan Bates at the Haymarket."

Police arrive and call an ambulance, and I am taken to St. Stephen's Hospital in Fulham, a guest of the British public health system by virtue of my student status. I am told I have a broken left arm, a smashed left elbow, and a left shoulder separation; am bandaged up and given some medication and a prescription for pain relief; and let go. When I wince as I step down from the gurney, I am told, "It's okay. It's your arm that's broken. Hmmm. Your right leg does look badly bruised, but there's nothing in the report. You can hail a taxi at the corner. Come back on Monday and we'll check the setting." I think grimly of the British stiff upper lip and painfully make my way to my home of one and a half days.

Sleep relieves me from the pain of being awake, and being awake relieves me from the pain of lying in bed. Sunday comes and goes in a haze of shock and pain. A strange ringing, two quick tones repeated over and over, wakes me on Monday morning. It seems to take forever for me to figure out it is my telephone. "Hello, this is Alan Bates. I just received your letter from the stage door manager. It has written on the envelope that you've been in some kind of accident. How are you?"

An unanticipated benefit of literacy! He has appreciated my letter, not a typical mash note but a serious inquiry about theater. We agree to meet in a month at the Lyric Hammersmith, where he will be performing in *Victoria Station*, to have lunch at the theater bar and to talk over some of my questions. I am amazed that he is so willing to respond to a complete stranger. His call bolsters me for the trip to the hospital, where I learn that the best treatment for my broken arm and shoulder separation is immobilization, whereas the best treatment for the smashed elbow, which took the brunt of my landing, is movement. Since simultaneous treatment is impossible, they immobilize my arm against my body and tell me to come back in four weeks, when they hope it will have set sufficiently so that we can begin moving my elbow, which is in danger of remaining permanently at a ninety-degree angle from the lengthy immobilization. Nothing is said about my swollen and blue right leg, though I mention I am having difficulty walking.

Thursday is the day of my first tutorial, and I am determined not to miss it. Stuffed with codeine, I face Harold Rosen. He is amazed that I have turned up at the tutorial. I am not as impressed with that as he is. After looking forward to these studies for three years, after having devoted almost every waking hour to preparing for this work, nothing is going to keep me away from any aspect of it, and particularly not from my first tutorial. Besides, I am in pain wherever I am. I might as well be putting my time to productive use rather than languishing in solitude. And so we start to talk about my assigned reading, a book on language by Gunther Kress. But I can't focus; I can't put sentences coherently together. The codeine will not allow me to articulate the ideas forming in my head. From an intellectual standpoint, the tutorial is a loss. However, during it Harold introduces me to two fellow students, who help me considerably through the next four weeks and who remain friends throughout and beyond my three-year stay: Jean Dunning, commuting from Leicester, who will be my tutorial mate under Harold's direction; and Yvonne LeGrande, from Melbourne, Australia, who, having herself been injured in a car accident two years earlier, understands exactly the kind of assistance I need and generously offers to come to my flat for the next few Saturdays to help me with cleaning, food shopping, and bathing.

Even more fortunately, as I am leaving the tutorial, Margaret Spencer (Meek), a senior lecturer at the Institute whose ideas on literacy are cited in several chapter epigraphs in this book, notices I am walking strangely and realizes something is very wrong. "Your leg is broken," she states, with what I learn to recognize as her habitual bluntness. "Why isn't it in a cast?" She immediately hustles me into her car, drives me straight to St. Stephen's Hospital, and insists that my right leg be X-rayed. We discover that it has indeed been broken in the accident, broken where the knee joint meets the long bone of the shin, and fractured just below that, at what they determine must have been the point of impact from the car.

Once my leg is bound, I can walk more easily, and I force myself to walk to St. Stephen's, a little over a mile away, three times a week for physiotherapy. My most basic coping mechanism for this stressful walk comes from my mother. Whenever I had felt sick or depressed as a child, she would urge me to visit the children in the Shriners Hospital who had been born without arms or legs. Then, according to her, I wouldn't feel so sorry for myself. Even as a child, I had been somewhat repelled by the idea of finding my own solace in someone else's misery. But after this accident, whenever I notice someone on the street with a permanent disability, I remember her words and feel relieved (and somewhat ashamed of this relief) by the realization that every day I am getting better.

And I am amazed at the helpfulness of strangers in one of the largest cities of the world. The only shoes flexible enough to accommodate my swollen foot are my sneakers, but I can't tie the laces with just one hand. On bad days, I can't even bend sufficiently to negotiate past the tongue and get my feet fully into them. I squiggle my toes as far into them as possible, struggle up the narrow steps of my basement flat to street level, and ask whomever I first meet to help me. Within a couple of days, one of the workmen renovating a house about four doors up the square has taken upon himself the responsibility to help me into my shoes and tie them, which he does with a generous flourish. Once, when he is busy, one of his workmates starts to tie my shoe. My regular shoe helper stops what he is doing, brushes his fellow worker's hand away, and says territorially, "I'm the one wot ties this lady's shoes, not you!" It is, perhaps, trivial, but it makes me feel less alone in this huge, strange city.

Similarly, it does not take the young newsboy whose stand is on the other side of the King's Road long to realize I am terrified to cross the street. Whenever he sees me waiting and waiting for a safe break in the traffic, he motions me to stay on the curb, and he darts across the street with my daily *Standard.*

Walking the mile to the hospital is not unbearably painful, but it seems to take forever for me to overcome my fear of crossing streets. The first part of the hospital treatment is like being in a posh salon—ice packs followed by electrical massage and then warm wax—but the physical exercises are excruciatingly difficult and painful. When the immobilizing binding is removed from my arm, we discover that my elbow has indeed locked at a ninety-degree angle and that the upper bone in my arm has fallen more than an inch below my shoulder socket. To begin the challenge of mobilizing the arm and tightening the shoulder connection, I have to lie flat on the bed and, holding an umbrella at both ends, raise both arms as high as I can. It is impossible; the hooked handle in my right hand zooms skyward while pointed end in my left hand barely moves.

I go home and devise a different plan of physiotherapy, one that focuses on the whole body. I put some rousing Rachmaninoff onto my tape recorder and begin to dance. Well, perhaps *dance* is not the most accurate word to describe my awkward and pained movements, but it is the principle of dance. It is based on the notion that all body movement is centered within the brain and spinal column. When you move an arm, that movement does not begin at the shoulder but somewhere deeper inside the body, somewhere more closely aligned with the spinal column and the part of the brain that controls movement. And when you move one arm, knowing that you intend to repeat that movement with the other arm, the whole network of nerve impulses that initiates the motion begins firing deep within the body's spinal system and moves outward to the extremities. I sweep out my right hand and try to trick my left hand into thinking it can match the movement. The neural movement from brain to shoulder should be the same right and left and, with repeated effort, should fire off those neurons and synapses a little farther down my arm each time. Of course, the left arm, rigid and bent, cannot match the movement of the right, but every time I try, it moves just a little bit better, and then I help it along with the right hand. Within six weeks of beginning mobility (ten weeks after the accident), exactly half the time predicted by the physiotherapist, my elbow is almost fully mobile and the shoulder is less than a quarter inch from the center of its socket. The leg injuries, being much less complicated, heal with much less conscious attention.

Because I am reading and writing about schooling and literacy while developing ways to heal my injuries, I understandably make connections between body and mind. I consider that the experience of dancing into full use of arm and leg can stand as a metaphor for literacy teaching and learning. Just as every fiber of my body wants to move, every child wants to learn to read and write. But, like the exercises with isolated bits of my body, bits of language decontextualized from the heart and soul of what kids do and hope to be able to do with language are too abstract, too cognitively distant from the learner's experiential center, to be helpful. Like the handle of my umbrella in my right hand, children may soar skyward with the small fragments of language they are learning and yet, like the pointed end in my left hand, remain unmoved and disengaged from the overall meaning of what they are learning. However, if the fragmented skills of language are united with something whole that is meaningful within their very essence, children will engage with their learning, will dance into literacy just as they dance into any experience they find rewarding.

There is only a limited amount of learning one can do sitting in a chair, reading alone, especially in a different culture. Therefore, my tutor, thinking I will learn more about the culture of education in England and especially inner-city London from listening to the research interests of fellow students, invites me to sit in on his master's class. One by one I hear fifteen British teachers show their commitment to the pedagogical, psychological, and physical needs of working-class kids. One is studying the problems experienced by gypsy children, travelers who spend only a few days or weeks at any one school. Another is looking at the oral and written language of working-class immigrants for whom English is not the mother tongue; another, at the marginalization of Bengali women hired as teachers' aides; another, at how many minority children's home dialects are neither acknowledged nor respected at school. One student begins his introduction in a knife-edged Liverpudlian accent with the words, "I'm working-class and proud of it!" Another begins telling about her study of the values expressed in working-class kids' writing by saying, "I've just finished the year at a smarmy middle-class girls' school. Those kids think they have problems? They don't know what problems are. Give me working-class kids any day. They're rough and they're tough, but they know what life is all about." I am confused. I have spent my life trying to situate myself in as refined circumstances as possible, trying to escape all that was stereotypically working-class, or lower-class, in my upbringing. Yet in this gathering of brilliant, dedicated teachers and scholars it seems that the working class is the class to be. My values of striving for upward mobility suddenly seem false and self-serving, and I feel diminished—and at the same time inspired—by their confidence, their dedication, and their commitment to what they hold to be most important about educating the upcoming generation of young people. I hope that I will develop some of their passion and commitment while I am here, but, even more, I begin to question many of my assumptions about class and even the goals that have brought me to London.

The first question they ask me when I introduce myself as a Canadian focuses on the problems of working-class kids in Canada. When I respond that people in Canada do not generally define themselves as working-class, that, right or wrong, people usually place themselves in the amorphously inclusive category of middle-class if asked, they rebut that I am naive and blind to the rampant class bias in North America. I am stunned, not expecting a frontal attack so soon on an issue I have not spent much time considering. It is the first of many cultural jolts that make me look at my Canadian culture very differently when I return. It is also the beginning of an ongoing interchange of ideas—frank, no holds barred—that forces me to look at how power structures in both Canada and Britain valorize the customs and language of an elite group of people while marginalizing those whose customs and language do not match or accommodate themselves to the standard. It is an entirely new way for me to view culture, language, and education.

Because the Institute's library has not yet been moved from its supposedly temporary location on the second floor of an old and grungy warehouse four blocks away from the Institute, my library of choice becomes the Reading Room of the British Museum. Almost every day I walk through the huge wrought-iron gates, between the cold stone lions, past the perpetual ice cream vendors, up the broad staircase, through the marble foyer, and into the grand circular reading room that had sheltered the thoughts of Marx and Joyce and Pound and Eliot and countless other writers of genius who had occupied those same seats of study. I take my regular place, caress the blue leather and golden mahogany carrel, breathe in deeply (but quietly), and lose myself in my reading. If I have a cold or a dry-throated cough and dare to pop a lozenge into my mouth, within seconds a kindly tap on the shoulder announces a spotless napkin held waiting to receive this forbidden indulgence. There are simply too many priceless manuscripts to risk a careless smear of sugary saliva. Overwhelmed by the somber beauty of the room, wondering how I have warranted the privilege of being able to study here,

I ask Harold if he ever got over his sense of awe. "You mean awe at working in that cadaverous Imperial Loot House?" he replies. "Only when you don't question whether you belong there will you really belong there." It is an enigmatic response, one that I still puzzle over from time to time. I have not yet decided whether I agree or disagree.

The first year in London is a blend of reading every day, writing every day, and talking with fellow students and my tutor once every two weeks. Doing a Ph.D. in Britain is, by and large, a lonely enterprise. In the first place, full-time doctoral students are rare, so there is not the regular graduate school organization that exists in North America. Without formal classes, it is difficult to find opportunities, other than conferences, to meet fellow researchers and to talk about the ideas one is reading and writing about. I am therefore grateful that my tutor pairs me with Jean Dunning, a secondary school teacher from Leicester, who has already begun work on her doctorate, a study of oral literacy specifically related to retelling stories.

Jean's approach to scholarship forces me to think about not only what we are both reading but also differing ways to approach interrelated concepts. When writing about her reading or about her interpretation of her students' retellings of stories, she says, "I just can't decide what to foreground and what to focus on. There is so much that is interdependent that I cannot start talking about one aspect without bringing in all the other ideas." We both know that in writing and talking about our reading we are dealing with the linear nature of written and oral language, which conflicts with the holistic nature of thought and experience. On the practical level, I have long since accepted the inevitability of the fact that one word must follow another, one idea another, in my writing, and have schooled myself to accept the concomitant oversimplification of ideas. But Jean refuses to accept it, and struggles endlessly with the tension between the two. That difference in our learning and writing styles forms a rich basis for dialogue about how to wrestle into written text all that we are learning about language.

I begin to question my too easy adoption of the triple-three approach to demonstrating learning that I learned in school: three main categories or overarching concepts, each with three ways to consider the concept, and each consideration buttressed with three examples or supporting details. By university, I had become adept at finding at least three main categories of response to any question asked on a test and presenting my (often very) limited knowledge as *the* three significant ways to consider the problem. That approach has served me well, but Jean's approach of trying to consider all possible angles and perspectives, though much more complex and prob-lematic, holds much more integrity than mine. Of course, she does not tell me this; we talk and talk, and the implicit integrity of her approach confronts my slick simplification and finds it wanting.

At the same time, Harold is also challenging my mode of writing, telling me that "you can get by in the academic world with this third person objective word-from-God North American dialect if you want to, but why would you want to." He goes on to tell me that ideas do not exist independently of someone's thinking, talking, or writing about them, and that I am an essential element of my interaction with and written presentation of ideas. I have to enter into my writing; I have to discover and proclaim my voice and my stance. This opens up a whole new understanding of literacy and of my, and my students', relationship to and with literacy.

Concurrently, John Dixon, a British scholar and educator, who has spent considerable time in Canada and whose work with teachers in Winnipeg has just resulted in his being made an honorary citizen of my home town, has taken an interest in my work. With Harold Rosen's agreement, he offers to serve as an informal tutor. Every second week, when they are in London, I spend a couple of hours in John and Mollie Dixon's Camden Town flat, talking over my recent reading and thinking, while John constructs diagrams of the structure of ideas in what I am saying. In essence, he maintains a concept map of my thinking over the three years I am in London. First he listens; then we talk. Sometimes he reads what I have recently written. After his first time reading one of my thought pieces, he looks up from his chair beside the carved Westmorland *kist* (chest) from Mollie's Cumbrian ancestors and says, "Sharon, you are allowing the form, the so-called academic essay form, to organize and limit your ideas. You are letting the form do your thinking for you. What if you have an idea that doesn't fit neatly into this form?"

These challenges to my thinking, the kind of thinking that has sustained me through school and university at a high level of achievement as far as grades go, force me to rethink what learning and writing are all about. In the meantime, I read everything I can lay my hands on about interrelationships among thought, language, learning, and teaching. Frequently I bemoan my growing appreciation of what teaching and learning are about while sitting alone in my chair rather than while teaching real kids in a real classroom. I itch to see these ideas in practice and look forward eagerly to the second year of my research, which will take me into schools, where I can talk with teachers and students about literacy: about their reading, writing, and learning.

9

Picking up the Hyphen

All choice of words is slang. It marks a class. . . . Correct English is the slang of prigs who write history and essays.

—George Eliot, *Middlemarch*

*H*ad I read that statement prior to my work on literacy in London, I would have found it funny and preposterous. However, the theoretical work of my first year and the field work of my second showed me that the statement is instead funny and profound. Historically, we have placed such a low value on some regional or cultural dialects that we have often blinded ourselves to the human insight articulated through them; conversely, we place such a strong value on so-called standard English dialect that we often assume wisdom in banality. This is not a new observation about language and literacy, although in 1984 it was a new realization for me. What deepened the realization was to meet face-to-face one who addressed me in "the slang of prigs" with words more characteristic of "male chauvinist pigs." It was probably a throwaway phrase, potentially a trivial moment, that became for me a conceptual watershed. It made me realize that feminist theory is not an abstraction that applies only to women of other countries or other cultures or other contexts or other times or any other other. It is embodied in the here and now and me.

I AM NOT ACCIDENT-PRONE. NO, I REALLY AM NOT. BUT I FOUND it very difficult to convince my tutor and fellow students at the London Institute of this when I began my second academic year once again wounded, this time with a black eye spreading in purple fury from my left eyebrow down to my chin.

My research school was a huge comprehensive school, part of the Inner London Education Authority. Twenty-five hundred students made for crowded halls at class changes, and madly dashing students did not combine well with a researcher unsure of her way in an unfamiliar maze of corridors. We were both traveling in the same direction in one of the less crowded hallways, he far behind me at breakneck speed, and I at my slow, dazed, feeling-lost tempo. Unaware of this male meteor hurtling toward me, I paused and turned, and in that brief second our cheekbones collided. We collapsed to the floor, he from obstructed momentum, I in a faint. I woke up on a cot in the nurse's room with an icepack on my cheek, under which a robin's egg was growing by the second.

I AM PREPARED FOR THE GOOD-NATURED JIBES FROM MY TUTOR and fellow students but not for the response of the Director for International Students. He is a distinguished-looking English gentleman, with silver hair and impeccable manners. I had met him the previous spring to receive the Vice-Chancellors Award for Promising Research from an Overseas Student, and was requested to meet him again this fall for a possible renewal of the award. At our first meeting, I considered him a good choice for his position, as his manner and interest made me feel welcome and secure. This initial impression is reinforced now until he remarks in his meticulous BBC accent, "I cannot resist commenting on your eye. What a beautiful shiner. Charming. Very sexy. Who gave it to you, may I ask? I almost wish I had given it to you myself." It is just a few words, possibly a comment to make me laugh. But the unexpected strangeness of his remark distracts me. It is a window into the concerns of gender that I had already encountered in my studies.

MY UNDERSTANDING OF LITERACY AT THAT TIME WAS NOT gender-specific. I knew that historically males had had better and longer access to schooling than females. I had just read Carolyn Steadman's *The Tidy House*, which explores how females' acculturation influences their literacy behavior, and had heard Dale Spender talk of women writers from earlier centuries whose writing had virtually been buried with them insofar as it had no access to publication. But I had not made any gender-based connections to my own literacy development. As I saw it, literacy had first of all enabled me to realize there were many ways to live my life beyond the limitations my parents and my immediate culture wanted to impose, and second, had empowered me to work toward whatever goals I envisioned. Also, I had just come to realize that it is not literacy itself, not reading and writing itself, but rather the capacity of literacy to transform us as human beings, and transform how we view ourselves in relation to the world in which we live, that is the basis of its power. Then the Director for International Students made his comment and startled me into some connections I should have made years earlier.

I began to think that possibly access to higher levels of literacy had been denied me not because I was adopted or was younger than my brother but because I was a girl. In my father's view, a girl was to look attractive and keep a clean home. In my mother's view, a girl had better be able to earn her own living by the time she was eighteen so her life would not be limited to just trying to look attractive and keeping a good home. I had not, before coming to London, perceived my mother as being trapped by her femaleness. Because she had gone to Africa for three years, from 1927 to 1930, first as governess to the children of the manager of International Harvester and then as a clerical worker for the Canadian Embassy, and from there had sailed to Europe, she had impressed me early in my life as self-directed and independent. She had returned to Canada in the midst of the Depression and had lived at her family's farm for almost two years before she found a job teaching in rural Manitoba. She had passed up the offers of a host of local farmboy suitors while waiting for the man who would promise her a house in the city, any city. My father, as she tells it, offered her a passport out of rural Manitoba and into cosmopolitan Baltimore. "I can forgive him anything because of that," she still assures me—and herself. She didn't like housework and didn't care to do laundry, so she had it done. Her husband, my father, didn't want her to work; she wanted to and did. He threatened to leave if she worked, and he did. As a child, I had interpreted all this behavior as individual people following their own paths, making their own life choices. I had never thought of it as my mother's trying to break away from gender-specific behavior and traditional expectations and my father's struggling to maintain male dominance.

One of the main features of literacy learning involves raising the level of generalization by classifying repeated or similar acts into an overarching category. It is probably the feature of learning most dependent upon social interaction and dialogue. I first became aware of the importance of knowing categories when I was six.

MOM IS READING ALOUD TO BILLY, DAD, AND ME THE LETTER that she has made Billy write to thank his Aunt Jean for Christmas money. Perhaps she doesn't think I know enough words in grade one to write a letter; for whatever reason, she hasn't asked me to write one, and I feel left out because for the first time Aunt Jean has sent me money too—and not just one dollar, the most I had ever held in my hand until then, but a whopping five dollar bill. So, I go upstairs, write my own letter, and bring it down for Mom to read. All is fine until she reaches the sign-off: "With love from your nefew, Sharon."

"A girl isn't a nephew," they all laugh.

"Well, what is a girl, then?" I demand, as though they are deliberately withholding information that would rescue me from my humiliation. It was a simple, predictable error of overgeneralizing the category. But even while realizing the importance of categories and learning about them in school, for some reason I did not tend to think categorically. I tended to respond to each person I met and to each event and crisis in my life as though it were fresh and new. That was brought home to me two weeks after my marriage, when we had Robert's mother, his brother, and his brother's wife over for Sunday dinner.

"You're very brave," his brother comments.

"Why?" I ask, wondering what on earth could have sparked that observation.

"Having all your in-laws together for dinner so soon," he replies.

In-laws! I am astonished and then overwhelmed. In my view, they are individual people—linked to my husband and now to me—whom I like and want to entertain. I had not, until that moment, gathered them together under the category "in-laws." That inability or unwillingness to categorize is why I neglected for so many years to consider gender as a cause for discrimination in my life. It would have required me to lump together a series of disparate and, I thought, unconnected incidents under an overarching umbrella of commonality, and that was a mode of thought that developed very slowly in me. It was also a mode of thought that required exposure to and awareness of the overarching category.

WE LEARN OUR CATEGORIES FROM OUR FAMILY, OUR SCHOOLING, and our culture—good and bad, right and wrong, what kind of people are good, what kind of behavior is appropriate, what kind of language is appropriate, what kinds of books are good, when to have sex, with whom, and under what conditions. These are all category-based, socially derived learning events in our lives. The process of developing one's categories is so culturally immersed it is almost invisible; the categories themselves seem a natural and inevitable part of us. That is why it so challenging to have to shift our categories—our acculturated ways of viewing the world and ourselves within that world. And yet, as I discovered almost every day of my London studies, shifting categories is what learning requires—demands—that we do.

The Director for International Students' comment shocked me into a reassessment of who I was, not as a scholar but as a bruised—and bruisable?—female, and provoked a shift in my understanding of how gender theory relates not just to literary criticism, to my students, or to women in developing countries or underprivileged classes but to me. Reluctant to test the waters of the legal profession again, I had not yet sought a divorce from Robert and so was still going by his surname of Wieler. Sometime during that walk from the director's office in Bloomsbury to my home in Chelsea, I realized I was no longer Sharon Wieler. Bearing in mind that I was still legally married, I decided the only way I could readily modify the name that represented me was to pick up a hyphen and include my maiden name of Hamilton. I left my home that morning as Sharon Wieler. I returned as Sharon Hamilton-Wieler.

The decision to add Hamilton was not an easy one. Memories of sitting on my bed upstairs while Mom, Dad, and Billy were arguing volubly downstairs, repeating to myself, "I am not a Hamilton; I am not a Hamilton; I am not a Hamilton; I don't know who or what I am but I am not a Hamilton," challenged the integrity of my resolution. And I was not blind to the fact that I was really only adding another paternally determined surname, that of a father who had changed my name to his when I was three and a half and had left when I was thirteen. Then I realized that I could call myself any name I liked; I could even revert to Karen Fleming if I wished. That realization made Hamilton-Wieler seem the best choice. It represented the totality of who I had been for thirty-seven of the forty years of my life—a kind of imperfect sum of an imperfect life.

Preoccupied with these musings, I walked the nearly three miles from London University to my flat in Chelsea doing something I had vowed I never to do: passing the architectural and horticultural delights of London without noticing and consciously appreciating them. Although there were many ways to connect Bloomsbury with Chelsea, my preferred path was to skirt Russell Square on Montague Street, walk past the columned southeast face of the British Museum down Museum Street across Holborn into

Shaftesbury, and round the corner to Cambridge Circus, dominated by the gothic splendor of the Palace Theater, home of Andrew Lloyd Webber's Really Useful Theater Company. Then I would meander past the bookshops and theater shops of Charing Cross Road to the National Portrait Gallery in Trafalgar Square; cross in front of the National Gallery, past Canada House (where I often felt shamed by picketers protesting Canadians' clubbing of baby seals), through those marble columns and majestic iron gates to The Mall, up through St. James's Park to Buckingham Palace, around Buckingham Palace Road to the great homes of Eaton Square, onto the King's Road, past Sloane Square, and then home. Not until I reached Sloane Square did I realize I had walked that amazing route so lost in thought that I had not seen anything. I vowed on the last ten minutes of that journey home to try to capture some of what I did every day in London.

Since most days of that second year in London I went not to the Institute but to my research school, I decided to write about that. And so I began my first piece of writing to be published under my new name. By the time I finished it, London was in the midst of winter.

It's London's coldest winter in almost thirty years, and as my alarm rings me awake at 7:00 a.m., the frosty air of my unheated Victorian flat assaults my face and hands. Ten minutes of brisk exercise warm me sufficiently to divest myself of all my nighttime layers of woollies and get into my daytime ones. It's like going skiing—woolen undervest, woolen tights, cotton and woolen shirt, woolen slacks, woolen sweater—I'm so layered I can barely move. A quick breakfast of muesli and coffee while watching BBC-1's Breakfast Time—essential if I want to know what tubes, trains, or buses have been canceled (today, for example, British Midland rail workers have called a one-day strike; in addition, two blizzards, one currently in Ireland, and the other on the Continent, will be criss-crossing England in a few hours, dropping several inches of snow and several degrees in temperature)—and I'm off to my research school.

The daily trip is in itself an adventure. My ten-minute walk up the King's Road to Sloane Square is too early to spot the punk rockers and Sloane Rangers who later will crowd the pavements but not too early to avoid having to weave warily amongst hordes of other Londoners on their way to work. Rushing past the seductive aromas of coffee shops and bake shops, I squeeze into one of the many tubes hurtling their way underground. Eight stops and fifteen minutes later, I'm at Cannon Street Station, in the heart of London, where I scan the electronic schedule high in the curved arches to see whether my train has been canceled, delayed, or rerouted. No problems today, just a slight delay of five minutes. It arrives disgorging hundreds of suburban commuters, each with newspaper and umbrella, and I crush through them, briefcase and tape recorder in hand, to find a place in one of the steamed-up, barely heated carriages (the faster intercity trains and more modern rolling stock are well heated, but southern region commuters rarely enjoy this advanced technology). We stutter along for twenty-five minutes, passing within view of St. Paul's Cathedral and Tower Bridge, down through Lewisham and Blackheath, to Falconwood Station, where I disembark together with close to two hundred sleepy-eyed adolescents, and complete the final ten minutes of my journey once again on foot.

Crown Woods School, located on the north downs of Kent, yet still part of the Inner London Education Authority, is a huge secondary comprehensive school with over 2,500 students aged eleven to nineteen and more than 160 faculty members. It offers a considerable variety of programs, from the workplace-oriented City and Guilds Department to the more academic Classics Department. My particular research involves me with twelve upper-sixth-form A-level students (roughly equivalent in age and educational preparation to our first-year university students) in six different subject areas: biology, English, geography, history, history of art, and sociology. I'm looking at the writing they do; at the contexts, particularly the language environment, in which the writing occurs; and the pedagogical issues that arise from the writing. This entails, in part, attending as many of the six classes as I can fit into my schedule, audiotaping the verbal exchanges, and taking field notes of nonverbal exchanges in order to gather as rich as possible a context for the writing. It also entails collecting all the written work done by my twelve students, including notes, rough drafts, tests, and exams, as well as holding formal and casual interviews with the students and their teachers.

Although I notice similarities between British and Canadian students, such as problems with organizing their study habits and anxiety about their future, I also perceive some differences. For one thing, very few sixth formers, particularly in this school, have jobs, ostensibly so they can devote more time to their studies. The sixth form itself is organized quite differently from our grade twelve, but because of the tremendous variety of options available to 16+ students, I'll just discuss the students I am observing. They are in the second year of the sixth form (hence upper sixth) and are taking from two to four A-level (advanced level) courses; the average is three. In July they will write external examinations based on their two years of work in these courses, examinations that will, to a significant extent, determine their prospects, whether for acceptance at a university or at a polytechnic (similar to our community colleges), or for potential employment. The pressure on the students and their teachers is enormous; it is evident in several of the classes I observe. Teaching in all areas except English is predominantly examination-oriented, a constraint that manifests itself quite strongly in the formal, information regurgitation writing frequently assigned to the students. Even so, most of the teachers I observe view themselves as teachers of the language as well as of the concepts of their respective disciplines, and help their students develop a repertoire of strategies for reading and writing appropriately within each disciplinary area. The focus is generally on how best to marshal evidence and deploy concepts and examples to establish a successful line of argument. Since English in this school includes a folder of writing done over the two years as one third of the final mark, however, considerable pressure is removed, and classroom writing reflects a pedagogy of exploration and discovery more than one of primarily marshaling and deploying information.

Today my first class is biology, and from 9:20 until 10:35 I learn the formulaic intricacies of photosynthesis and how, in science, results and conclusions can be correct or accurate but not necessarily "true." Break time, then, for the entire school (except the staff on hall duty as it is too cold for the students to go outdoors). More than one hundred teachers converge on two beleaguered tea ladies who sell tea and coffee at sixpence a cup and biscuits (cookies) freshly baked in the school kitchens at three pence each. Twenty minutes later I'm in a sociology class, listening to a discussion of changing family structure from a Marxist-feminist viewpoint. Then lunchtime, and after collecting some sociology exams to photocopy and analyze, and arranging for a private interview with one of my twelve students to discuss one of her writing projects, I go to the tiny English department office to munch the tomato sandwich and orange I brought from my flat. I could have eaten in the Lodge (the dining room for teachers, the sixty students who live in residence at the school, and any other students wanting a hot lunch) a full meal including a hearty but stodgy English pudding for only ninety-six pence (about $1.50), but, as usual for this time of year, I'm trying to lose my Christmas indulgence. While four of us bemoan the wretched weather over our sandwiches, we can't help overhearing the sympathetic and encouraging remarks of the English head of department who has just been tearfully informed by one of the three novice (first-year) teachers in the department that she doesn't want to be a teacher anymore.

Novice teachers are treated quite differently in English schools than they generally are in Manitoba schools. In the first place, in this particular school, they are given a significantly lighter teaching load, just over two

thirds of a regular load, and have no tutor group (home room) to adminis-
ter. In addition, they are assigned to a senior teacher or head of department
who regularly (two to three times a week) listens to them, works with
them, helps and counsels them. It's a very supportive system, but even
so, as evidenced today, the pressures of teaching still exact their toll on
the young teacher.

At 12:30, the tea ladies are again in place in the staff room, with
more fresh biscuits, cakes, and chocolate bars, and then, at 1:05, I'm off
to history. We're learning about the Irish famine of 1845 and of how half
of the population of eight million lived on only potatoes. I think back to
last night's newscast announcing the increasing shortage of fresh vegetables, both domestic and imported, since this frigid air stream is affecting
the Continent even more than Britain, and mentioning that the only
vegetable in sufficient supply is the hardy potato. A dozen shrill pips
announce change of class at 2:20 p.m., and I struggle through a maze of
narrow halls crowded with hundreds of pushing, shoving bodies to my
final class of the day, English. I feel more at home in the English classroom,
having taught the subject for seventeen years in Manitoba and, because
of the teacher's penchant for group discussion, am as much a participant
here as an observer. Today we are continuing our oral reading of *King
Lear* and discussing quotations from Act I that indicate salient features
of the main characters. The 3:30 pips announcing the end of the school day
interrupt a lively exchange of opinion about whether Edmund, although a
villain in deed, is not somewhat maligned in critical theory, in a manner
similar to Richard III. Damian Tambini, one of the students in my study,
gives me the rough notes and preliminary drafts of his most recent essay,
I speak with Rebecca Sandles, another of my students, about her writing
journal; I borrow a copy of Virginia Woolf's *A Room of One's Own* to
trace intertextual features in Damian's essay titled "A Conclusion of One's
Own"; and I'm through for the day—in school, at least.

The journey home is not completely the reverse of the outbound
journey. Instead of going straight across the Thames from London Bridge
to Cannon Street, we shunt alongside the river, past the flame-topped
monument marking the start of the great fire of London, past the cultural
conglomerate of the South Bank: the National Theater, Hayward Gallery,
the National Film Theater, Queen Elizabeth Hall, and the Royal Festival
Hall, to cross the Thames in the ghostly shadow of Big Ben and the towers
of Westminster as we chug into Charing Cross Station. From there it's a
short walk down Villiers Street, with its video shops, pubs, the house
where Kipling lived for two years, and the best (if my nose is right) fish
and chip place in London, Johnnie's Fish Bar, to the Embankment.

Each of the London Underground stations has its distinctive character, but for me the Embankment in the mid-1980s, not yet transformed into the glitzy windowed dome that now dominates the Thames skyline, is the most poignant. It is one of the several refuges of London's down-and-outers, those with no work, no money, and no homes. Even in the bitterly cold weather, they sleep rough in a sort of cul-de-sac in front of the station. In front of their piles of tattered blankets and sleeping bags are hawkers selling newspapers, flowers, fruit, and vegetables. Inside the station door is a bake shop selling the creamiest, wickedest pastries one could imagine. I pass this plethora of human activity, step onto one of the west-bound tubes, get out at Sloane Square, and I'm almost home.

The drop in temperature forecast in the morning is quite apparent, and although as yet there is no snow, the sky has an eerie whiteness in contrast to the enveloping darkness at street level. I walk as briskly as I can down the always crowded King's Road, descend carefully the steep 140-year-old steps to my basement flat, and unlock my barred wooden door with a huge brass key, hoping to find some interesting mail.

Fortunately, I do (living so far away from home, family, and friends makes me very dependent upon the post). I make myself a cup of hot Earl Grey tea to warm me while I read my letters and plug in my new portable fire (electric heater) for the allotted ten minutes (all I can afford). Soon it's time for the six o'clock news, which I watch as I feast on a bowl of hearty homemade vegetable soup. The pound is down again (a blessing for me, since my funding is primarily in Canadian dollars, but a curse for those who suffer from the concomitant rise in interest rates); the long-suffering miners, impoverished after ten months of striking, are gradually being forced back to work by economic pressures without any material gains to show for their torment; Piccadilly Circus is being sealed off from all traffic because of a suspected gas leak; and people and animals all over Great Britain are dying because of the cold—a grim picture. Supper and the news over, I clean up my toy kitchen: my fridge is smaller than the minibars you find in hotel rooms, my hot water comes from a two-liter tank I heat up each time I want any, and I've no counter at all.

And then the difficult part of the research begins. I go over my tapes and field notes, summarizing the salient bits and filing, hopefully in efficiently retrievable fashion, all the papers and data I've collected. Harold Rosen, my tutor, has suggested that I take a problematic or unusual student text and do a meta-analysis of ways of interrogating it that would be most helpful in raising pedagogical issues, so I work on that for a while. My ability to concentrate on creatively productive work quickly wanes, however, as the evening progresses, and I finish working in a more receptive mode, reading some recent but as yet unpublished work of the linguist and anthropologist Dell Hymes on communicative competence.

By 9:30 I'm mentally exhausted and so indulge myself in a dose of Americana by watching Quincy on the telly. Then, fortified with a healthy dose of Bailey's Irish Cream, I crawl into my igloo, plug in my electric fire for the allotted ten minutes, and fall asleep after my nightly chapter of Umberto Eco's *The Name of the Rose*, dreaming of that twentieth-century blessing, central heating.

10

Oh, to Be in Bloomsbury!

"Human nature changed in or about December 1910," Virginia
Woolf asserted as she attempted to pinpoint the coalescing spirit of
twentieth-century sensibility. She went on in a later essay to inquire,
"Have I the power of conveying the true reality? . . . Or do I write
essays about myself?"

A literacy narrative is probably the most unabashedly self-
conscious essay of self, though all writing is inevitably
invested with the writer. Woolf's question is not a real
question but rather a pointer to the inadequacy of language to
wrestle into black type on white paper anything but a subjectively
selective verisimilitude of reality. It helps us understand her assertion about human nature changing in (or about) December 1910.
It also enables me to write that I left London a different person
from the linguistically, culturally, and politically ignorant thirty-
nine-year-old woman who had arrived there three years earlier.
I had come with a professional but unfocused interest in language,
literacy, and learning, and I left with a passionate investment in
a more class-conscious perspective of human ecology and language, a stronger sense of the people and places I encountered,
and a stronger sense of who and how I was becoming. My human
nature changed in or about the years 1983–1986, but it was more

than just the acquisition of a doctoral degree that caused the change. As Woolf, in one of her most cited references, states that a woman needs a room of her own and five hundred pounds a year in order to write, I needed time to think, space to walk about and think in, and the emotional, cultural, and intellectual stimulation of fellow sojourners in the world of language and literacy to help me shape and focus my thinking, and to help me define who and how I wanted to be.

BLOOMSBURY AT LAST. WITHIN A BLOCK OF THE HOME OF VIRGINIA Woolf. Within two blocks of T. S. Eliot's former publishing house. Within three blocks of the British Museum. Finally I have become eligible for one of the highly prized and hotly contested Institute flats. I set up house in my Woburn Square flat and buy a new-to-the-market Amstrad computer, which after two weeks of continued frustration trying to learn how to operate it from a manual that has over fifty errors and omissions, I name BOF (Boring Old Fart).

Beginning to write my dissertation is a daunting prospect. I dither and stall for almost a week before I figure out the plan that will sustain me. I set up two inviolable rules: I cannot go to bed until I have written five pages, and I cannot eat breakfast the next morning until I have revised them. After about a month of lurching through my ideas in five-page spurts, I finally begin to develop some fluency and can often write seven or eight pages in a day. These extra pages I "bank" until I have ten, fifteen, or twenty "extras" and then I spend them on a two-, three-, or four-day holiday.

These brief holidays became real adventures. I take the first tube going to either Charing Cross or Victoria Station, look up at the huge board in the rotunda, and choose the next train going to any coastal city. I make my way downhill from the train station to the seashore, select an economical bed-and-breakfast, and walk. I love Hastings for its two-mile-long seawall, against which the waves pound and crash. I love Penzance for its winding sandy shore leading to St. Michael's Mount, an island or a peninsula depending on the time of day. I love Brighton for its seedy beach pavilions and boardwalk piers, with fortune tellers and hawkers of everything from seashells to tattoos. I love St. Ives for its winding roads and picturesque fishing boats nestled colorfully in its hill-encased harbor. I love them all and work all the harder to earn my two-, three-, and four-day jaunts to the seaside.

After eight and a half months of this regime, I am one chapter away from completing my thesis. I have written that chapter, the opening one, three times already but have been advised by my tutor each time to "put it aside, think it through, and begin again." In the dissertations I have read, the first chapter has seemed primarily a review of the related literature, and that's how I have conceived the purpose of that first chapter. But Tony Burgess, who has replaced my now retired tutor Harold Rosen, cautions me about bringing such a reductionist stance to any genre and particularly to the first chapter of a doctoral thesis. "This is where you earn your right to enter the conversation of scholars in your field," he tells me. "You want to make reference to significant reading that is related to your research, but do it in such a way that out of your discussion emerges your research question as the inevitable, only possible, and absolutely essential next step in exploring your field." He then offers me one of the most significant images that I still draw upon and share with my writing students: "Think of your task in this opening chapter as setting out on a journey with a group of strangers. You need to reach out to these strangers, your readers who will have differing ideas, differing stances, and differing ways of considering writing and learning in the academy. Think of having to draw them in close to you and to your ideas, and then, once you have drawn them all in, you can set off together down the path that you have determined."

It is a challenge that takes me several tries. I finally construct a path through the literature that does indeed lead inexorably and inevitably to the body of my research. I am almost done with my fourth and what will be my final version of the first chapter when a phone call at three o'clock in the morning threatens my plans. It is my mother. "David is in the hospital. In the intensive care unit. He has overdosed on drugs. You need to come home immediately."

Come home immediately. It seems an easy, straightforward request. But I am four days away from completing my thesis (if all goes well), which is already scheduled to be taken to the bookbinders on the fifth day. I have an appointment on the sixth day for exploratory surgery on my bladder, which has been bleeding increasingly profusely for the past six weeks. Four days later, I am to pick up the bound copies of my thesis and send them to my examiners in preparation for my viva voce (orals) in six weeks, and four days after sending out my thesis, I am scheduled to speak at an international conference in Ottawa, Canada, after which I will be flying home to Winnipeg for a couple of weeks before returning to London for my viva. Should I drop everything, lose almost a thousand dollars on the tickets already purchased, risk delaying my surgery, postpone the completion of my thesis, and try to get a flight home? Or should I follow my schedule?

It is a question that every mother (and probably father) has to contend with more than once as their children maneuver through life's perils, and it is a question that I feel I have failed to respond to appropriately every time it has been asked of me. David has an uncanny knack of needing me exactly at times when I am right in the midst of unchangeable schedules, external demands, or general anesthesia. Three times during the three years prior to my coming to London I had had outpatient surgery, and every time, within hours of my coming home and falling into the deep sleep assisted by post-op pain killers, the telephone rang. David had fallen at a party, required stitches, and needed his guardian parent to pick him up from the hospital. Unable to drive in my groggy condition, I had to call someone in the middle of the night to pick me up and take me to the hospital so that I could bring my teenage son home.

These recollections flash through my mind as I try to figure out what to do. At last I decide to call the hospital and determine David's actual condition. That is impossible from the hall phone outside my flat. It is the old kind that accepts only ten-pence coins, and I would need more than a hundred coins for my call. I pull on some warm clothes, hit the cold 3:30 a.m. air, and shiver my way to the Russell Hotel, three blocks away, to use one of their warm, quiet lobby phones, which will accept a prepaid phone card. After pleading negotiations with the Russell Hotel doorman, understandably reluctant to let a sleepy-eyed nonresident into the fine marble foyer in the middle of the night, and a few false starts—my mother has not recalled the right hospital—I locate the intensive care unit of the Misericordia Hospital in Winnipeg and learn that David is out of danger, recovering just fine, and likely to be released in a couple of days. I could speak with him, but he is sleeping.

After consulting in the morning with my tutor, who advises me to keep to my schedule since David is recovering, I call my mother to tell her I will be home in three weeks. While the decision is fairly straightforward, it brings back all the feelings of guilt and inadequacy that I felt when David was growing up. What would I have done if he had not been out of danger? I think I would have flown home immediately, but then again I'm not sure. Is something wrong with me as a mother? Most mothers I know of my generation put their children absolutely, unconditionally first. And I don't have any idea what to do with the notion that David has overdosed on drugs. The doctor is vague over the telephone about the nature of the problem, but it seems completely out of character for David, who, as far as I know, doesn't smoke and drinks only to be sociable at parties. How am I supposed to balance these worries with the need to focus and finish? And as a mother, what am I supposed to do? What is the right thing to do?

I finally get hold of David and discover that his alleged overdose has been, to use Twain's phrase, "greatly exaggerated." During one of his recurring bouts with pneumonia, he had neglected to take his medication, had then taken three—perhaps four, he isn't sure—times the prescribed dosage, had felt dizzy and fallen, and had consequently gone to the emergency ward of the nearby Misericordia Hospital in a dazed and incoherent state. Unfortunately, the doctors decided that David had deliberately taken too much medicine and had tried to commit suicide. For two days they badgered him to confess his disturbed psyche before finally realizing that he was simply absent-minded on occasion, not suicidal.

With relief, I complete my thesis on schedule and carry the five hundred and forty-five pages to the official bookbinders of London University, a wonderfully Dickensian establishment near Camden Town, with a huge brass knocker on the door, a quietly bustling interior, and a bespectacled clerk to process my order with polite but tediously slow inefficiency. With my London stay coming to a close, it is a scene that I absorb to the fullest.

Six weeks later, the words hang in the air. I want to grab them, clasp them to me, shout them out to the world, but they hang in the air, inaccessible for the next three hours. "Congratulations! You have earned the Ph.D. from London University. Now, let's sit down and chat about your work." Of all the possible ways to begin the doctoral viva voce, those words represent the best way. The morning began inauspiciously with a call from Tony Burgess, my tutor, canceling our pre-viva coffee and chat because of a last-minute meeting with my internal and external examiners. His words, "You have nothing to worry about," did nothing to assuage my mounting fear. Would I be denied the doctorate? Would I be offered the less prestigious Master of Philosophy degree? Would I have major revisions requiring another trip to the bookbinder's, more delays, and another viva in a few months? These were all very common possibilities, and the knowledge that my former tutor, Harold Rosen, had failed two of the three candidates for whom he had served as external examiner the previous year, one of whom had been a close and admired colleague of his, put a sharp edge on my fear. Whereas North American dissertation defenses are primarily pro forma, European vivas are the moment of truth, the moment of acceptance into or denial of the privileges of the professoriate. And so I sit with those words hovering in the air, tantalizing me but eluding my grasp until the conclusion of the viva. We converse about literacy and about my thesis, James Britton, Margaret Spencer (Meek), Tony Burgess, and I, and then I snatch the words of acceptance out of the air, stuff them into my sense of self, and leave London as Dr. Sharon Hamilton-Wieler. It is a mouthful, a fine-tasting mouthful.

11

The Lucky One

"We read to know we are not alone," says one of C. S. Lewis' students in the movie *Shadowlands*. We find ourselves, or some part of ourselves, in the strangest places in literature. Sometimes it's frightening, if we see a part of ourselves we have not yet learned to tolerate or to change. Often it's reassuring, when we discover we are not the only ones who have suffered that particular kind of pain, or have thought that kind of thought, or have done that kind of deed. Occasionally, it's inspiring, when we see that others like us can achieve, or can love and be loved, or can contribute something meaningful to the world.

I have known for a long time that "we read to know we are not alone." Only recently have I discovered what everyone around me seems to have known always: we maintain family units to know we are not alone, even when we feel alone within that family. That discovery was highlighted for me because I was already forty-two when I learned that I had eleven siblings, two of whom had died shortly after birth, and then met six of them. Their blood was my blood. That was not a truth I felt with any intense emotion. But their experience was my experience, at least in part, and that did hit me emotionally. Being intellectually aware that I was and am not alone is not the same as emotionally rolling in both the muck and the flowers of it.

SEPTEMBER 1986. I AM AT THE HOME OF MICHAEL SIMPSON, my brother. He is two and a half years younger than I am, smaller of bone, and he looks and seems very pleasant. No striking family resemblance leaps out. He is explaining how my call to the *Winnipeg Free Press* three years earlier had completed the puzzle that he and Colin, also my brother, had been piecing together for several years, unaware of each other's endeavors until Colin's story became public.

This is my first meeting with Michael, and he is telling me about my siblings: Jackie, the eldest, whom I have already met, whose father had been a soldier stationed near Winnipeg during the Second World War; me next, and then Susan, the only two of us who share the same father, Jack Fleming; then Michael, who holds that Jack is also his father, though Jack contends that Michael was conceived the winter that Irene was in the Portage La Prairie jail. Then there is Colin, whose father, a British pilot in the Royal Air Force, had not been allowed to adopt him; Hope, whose physical similarity to Colin in the photograph Michael shows us suggests that her parentage may be the same as Colin's; Lincoln, who will be arriving shortly, and then three others whose last name of Simpson implies, though does not guarantee, that they were all fathered by Irene's second husband.

Just as Michael finishes telling me about all these people Irene had brought into the world, Susan arrives. This meeting at Michael's place is not only to inform me about all my siblings but also to enable many of us to meet each other. Looking at Susan is like looking into a mirror, the distorting kind of mirror that changes shape and size but cannot falsify the soul that peers through the eyes. Susan looks exactly like me—identical bone structure, particularly noticeable in her face, the same height of 5'7", and the same almost-sallow complexion and pale green eyes—except that her weight is over three hundred pounds, her teeth are rimmed with brown decay, and her eyes tiredly dare me to challenge her relentlessly bitter state of mind and sense of self. Susan's story is discomfiting. After being juggled for several years between foster homes and Irene's home, she was finally placed in a long-term foster home, was raped by her foster father when she was sixteen (or raped on the way home from school by some unidentified person, and then beaten and kicked out of her home by her foster father— the story changes from first telling to second telling), and then bore a son of that rape. Married to a kindly older man a few years later, she bore him three children and then declared that she was a lesbian. As a result of that declaration, she lost husband and children, except for her son of the rape, now in his early twenties, with whom she is still living, both on welfare. Her home, some rooms in an older boarding house, is four blocks away from where I am living—in the same apartment block on Wellington Crescent where I had lived before I left for London. Her story explains the tired bitterness in her eyes.

I understand why I feel sad hearing this. But I cannot understand why I feel uncomfortable, almost guilty. Why can I not reach out to her and hold her and try to find some words of comfort? I seem to be inadequate in this department of feelings, just as I was when I met Jackie at age eighteen.

While Susan is telling her story, Colin arrives. His eyes, a clear blue in contrast to the pale green of Susan's, glitter with the excitement of the moment as he settles into the telling of his tale. Like Susan, he had been shunted back and forth between foster homes and Irene's home, and like Susan, he bears the scars of rape, beatings, and torture by cigarette burns with bitterness. This bitterness clouds his eyes when he tells of how he wants to love someone, marry, and raise a family. But he cannot. Colin is a clown. He is Ronald McDonald. He relates to people through a mask. When he is not Ronald McDonald, he is a coach for his local community club, a hockey coach in winter and a baseball coach in summer. He relates to people through his uniform. Yet he is not wearing a uniform or a mask now—or at least not a mask that I know him well enough to recognize—and he is relating to us. Physically, he is small and tightly wound, a nervous bundle that seems ready to explode. He radiates a field of energy that seems to warn, "Keep away from me," at the same time that it implores, "Like me. Be with me." He seems very easy to like; he seems to really want to be liked.

Susan scares me. Is it because we are the closest in blood and I have her essence inside me, a caustic essence I want to deny rather than embrace? But Colin worries me. He worries me because he combines so many paradoxes. He is intensely bitter yet warmly radiant with the joy of this meeting. He sincerely wants to be close to people but cannot sustain a relationship. He loves but cannot make love. He is enraged at his treatment by the Children's Aid Society, still enraged after more than thirty years. That's a long time to contain rage. And then I identify my worry: that rage seems ready to explode, probably not in a way to hurt others but very possibly in a way to hurt Colin.

Then Jackie arrives with Lincoln, one of the youngest, still in his early twenties, adopted by a Mennonite family who did not want him to come to this gathering today. Lincoln is calm and gentle, like Michael, and in fact looks like a younger version of Michael. Perhaps they have the same father. No one knows. Lincoln says he has come especially to meet me, since they have already all met each other during the three years between my telephone call and this reunion. He sits at my knee, like an acquiescent puppy, and says little about his life story. He lets us know, however, that his adoptive parents do not want him to pursue this Lawrence-Fleming-Simpson family connection after today.

Jackie has come with her husband all the way from Toronto. Her red hair and pale green eyes are familiar landmarks in this sea of strangers, and we have a sense of not having to forge yet another whole new relationship. We sit side by side and talk about our families and our children. In the meantime, Michael and his wife serve delicious hors d'oeuvres and home-baked delicacies. It all seems so normal, so incredibly normal. To any outside observer, we would seem to be an ordinary family chatting about our jobs, our children, and the day-to-day trivia of our existence. What unfolds, however, as each person unwraps the layers of civilized veneer, is a tale of unhealed scars and bruises that takes this gathering beyond the realm of the ordinary.

I am cast in a completely unaccustomed role. My life, which I had found so fraught with challenge and bias, has been the easiest of the lot. For years these individuals have considered me to be the lucky one. The rumor was that I had been adopted by a wealthy and loving American family who had taken me down to the States. It was that rumor that led Colin to have his story published without locating me, since he believed he had found all the siblings located in the Winnipeg area. Despite that misunderstanding, it seems evident to them that I am happy with my current life and bear no (visible) scars, as many of them do.

I am the lucky one.

At one moment, the spotlight turns on me, and they all wait to hear my story. My mind races through my history, trying to figure out whether to respond to their expectations of a happy, well-adjusted childhood or to conjure up my own wretched memories. I decide to do neither. I am both comfortable and uncomfortable with the unanticipated role of being the lucky one. It seems simultaneously a lie and a truth. It captures the ambivalence that has plagued me since I first arrived at the Hamiltons.

I HAD KNOWN RIGHT FROM THE START THAT I WAS TO BE GRATEFUL for being allowed to live with the Hamiltons because if they had not taken me, probably nobody else would have, and I would likely have lived out the Children's Aid Society's low expectations of me. The Hamiltons were kind, good people, my life savers and shapers. And I think I always knew that their intentions were good. What I could not understand was their unquestioned, and in their eyes absolutely unproblematic and undenied, stratifying of Billy, me, and Joe.

Joe was obviously at the bottom of the hierarchy, even though he was their officially documented foster child. As soon as he left the household, when I was about five years of age, to find work and then to marry, he was out of our family life. He was not part of our Christmas celebrations; I have no idea when his birthday is; there was no familial interchange. I don't think he was ever referred to as Billy's or my brother or foster brother. He was just Joe. I doubt that any of our neighbors ever realized that Joe was a foster son and not some kind of hired hand. Yet he was always grateful to the Hamiltons for having brought him to Canada after his parents were killed, always polite to my mother and father even when my father was not always polite to Joe, and if ever my mother needed help with something around the house, she knew she could count on Joe to see to it. She still can. And she is very proud of Joe's successes in life and pleased (though not proud— it's not her way) with the role she was able to play in enabling some of those successes to occur.

At the other end of the hierarchy was Billy, their "real" son, the son of their flesh and blood. Whenever Dad left on one of his business trips, he would warn Mom, "That boy better be alive and healthy when I return, or you better not be here." I could never quite figure out that comment, because Mom always took good care of Billy, and Dad was generally not a mean, threatening type of person. It was just that Billy was everything to him. One time I asked Dad, "What if I'm not alive and healthy when you return?" and he looked at me strangely, almost as though he had forgotten I was there. He answered by ordering me outside, telling me that "children shouldn't be hanging around when adults are talking and then they won't overhear things they shouldn't."

Mom and Dad had differing plans for Billy. Dad wanted him to join his contracting firm of Ducharme and Hamilton, and Mom wanted him to do well in school and become a man of business. I have no idea what Billy wanted, if indeed he had ever planned beyond their planning. The only thing that comes to mind is his tremendous admiration for Uncle Joe, my father's brother, a retired miner who built a wood cabin with squatter's rights on the edge of Nicola Lake in British Columbia and fished every day he possibly could. Spoonfishing like Uncle Joe was the closest Billy ever came to expressing a desire for a particular occupation, other than working as a general contractor like his Dad, as far as I know. Our household functioned on orders about and limitations on hopes and dreams, not conversations about them. Mom's and Dad's hopes competed for Billy's time and attention. Dad thought it fine to take Billy out of school for a couple of weeks to work on a hospital or high school contract in Sioux

Lookout or Emerson or some other town miles away from home. Mom spent hours each school-day evening with Billy, trying to help him learn his English and his math. I think that's one explanation for my doing so well in grammar: every night, as I lay upstairs in bed, I would hear them at the kitchen table: "The boy hit the ball. *Boy* is the subject. What's the verb? What's the object?" And I would whisper the answers to myself, wondering whether Billy really couldn't get it or was just playing dumb to irritate Mom.

But they had no plans for me, and so never competed for my time and attention. Mom thought that all girls should know how to play the piano and that dancing lessons would strengthen my legs, so I ended up the beneficiary of lessons in both from the time I was six until I completed junior high school. She also thought that all girls should be employed by the time they were eighteen, so she gave me the choice of one year at a teachers college or a business college, though I wanted neither. I had my own plans, but nobody in my family was interested in them.

Coincidentally, just days before this meeting at Michael's, Billy had also declared me to be "the lucky one." His reason: "They never promised you anything. Dad promised me a house, an education, a car, a great job, money—Dad promised me everything, and so I grew up expecting it, and ended up disappointed on every count. They promised you nothing, and so you never expected anything. You grew up knowing that you would have to work for everything that you wanted. You're the lucky one. You knew exactly what you needed to do."

The lucky one.

It's a question of perception and misperception and truth all mixed up in the chaos of how we negotiate the events and circumstances of our lives. As an adult, I can appreciate the perspective of my blood siblings and my adopted sibling. I even *feel* lucky after listening to all their stories, although it is a sad kind of lucky, the kind I used to feel when my mother would tell me to compare myself with the children at the Shriners Hospital born with no arms and legs. Why, as a child, did I feel bound by the chains of such wretched misery? Was a change of attitude all that I had needed to have been happy from the time I was adopted?

In *Hamlet* we read, "There is nothing either good or bad but thinking makes it so. . . . I could be bounded in a nutshell and count myself a king of infinite space. . . ." I suppose I could have bound myself within the Hamilton family and counted myself fortunate, except that I wanted something that they could not understand. Not just university, though I felt university was the key to my achieving the kind of life I wanted. I wanted a way of life different from the life I was living—a life without contention, without arbitrary constraints, without feeling second-best, a life where I could make choices and be in charge. Even now, my mother will say, "I didn't know there was anything after grade twelve for a girl except normal school or secretarial school. I just didn't know." How can I fault someone for not knowing? How can I excuse someone for not listening? How can I not appreciate the person who introduced me to new worlds—by reading me stories, poems, myths, and legends, by telling stories of her life in Africa and of her subsequent ocean voyage to Europe, by tantalizing my mind, heart, and soul to know more, travel more, and be more—even if she did not acknowledge that these new worlds were possible for me?

THESE THOUGHTS WORM THEIR WAY THROUGH MY MIND AS MY siblings speak of their grief and bitterness. No, not all my siblings. Michael and Jackie are impressive in their calm equanimity, warm, generous natures, and sincere caring for all their new-found family. I decide to accept everyone's designation of me as the lucky one and tell safe and funny stories of my adventures in London. No point dredging up sad memories.

On the way home, I stop at a florist and confectioner to purchase a dozen red roses and a box of Godiva chocolates for my mother. The lucky one should be magnanimous.

In my wallet I have a gift from Michael, a card with the work address and telephone number of Jack Fleming, my birth father. At home I take it out and put it on the table, look at it, and consider my options. Michael had flown to Calgary in the hope of being acknowledged as Jack Fleming's son. He had been devastated by Jack's rejection of him, as a son, not as a person. I know that I will not put myself into any position of rejection that I can avoid. I could write him, although with only a work address that could be risky. I could telephone him, but again, the kind of call I would be making might not be appropriate in a work situation. And then there are my "real" parents, the Hamiltons, who have looked after me most of my growing-up years. Although my mother has always been curious about my birth family and enjoys talking with Michael over the telephone, I have a sense that she might not be overjoyed by my pursuing the connection too energetically. I am sure my adoptive father, who spends a couple of months of every year in Winnipeg even though he has an American wife in Los Angeles, would not approve. Where do my loyalties lie? Is loyalty even the appropriate issue with which to concern myself?

So I put the card back into my wallet and do nothing.

A YEAR AND A HALF LATER MY FATHER, MY HAMILTON FATHER, DIED. He had been home to Winnipeg for Christmas, had told Mom he was going to settle his American affairs—business and domestic—and return in a couple of months to live out his days with her in Winnipeg, had required surgery in Los Angeles, and had never left the hospital. Billy, once the apple of his eye, took a bitter pride in writing an obituary that occupied less than a column inch of space. I felt the grief of losing a father who had just seemed to discover his right place in life but had run out of time to arrive there.

Two years after that, I wrote Jack Fleming the following letter: "If the name Karen Agnes Fleming, born July 1, 1944, means anything to you, I want you to know that I am Karen, now Sharon Hamilton-Wieler, alive and healthy and happily working as an English professor in Indianapolis. If you choose not to reply to this letter, I will respect that decision and will not contact you again. However, if you wish to write or telephone me, I will be very happy to hear from you." I considered that to be sufficiently nonthreatening.

He wrote back an amazing letter: "My dear, darling daughter Karen. Of course, you mean something to me. You are my first-born. I named you. I chose 'Karen' and 'Agnes' because they are the names of two very precious people in my life." He went on to tell me how thrilled he was to hear from me and, most surprising of all, he said, "I love you very, very much."

I didn't know how to react to such an outpouring. How could he love me? He didn't even know me. That one letter contained more terms of endearment than I had ever heard from my adoptive parents in all the years I was growing up. Doesn't love have to be earned? Does just being alive entitle me to love from my parents? Or was he just using the words he thought he ought to use? I had worked so hard to try to earn or merit love from parents and husband, and by this virtual stranger I was being granted the status of "loved one" simply for being alive and being his daughter.

We corresponded for the next three years. He wrote marvelous letters, telling me of his early days in Plum Coulee, a small town in southern Manitoba, of the Depression that yanked him out of school and led to his running away from the poverty-induced hardships in his large family, of joining the armed forces, being furloughed in Winnipeg, and meeting and being seduced by Irene, my birth mother. I looked forward to each installment of his story and reciprocated with some of mine. And then the letters stopped. Instead, he sends me cards for my birthday and for Christmas, beautiful and loving cards but no match for his letters.

I was fascinated by those letters, many of them ten to twelve pages long, mostly because of the story they told, but also because of the fluency and quality of the writing. Jack Fleming had not completed the sixth grade yet wrote as fluently and comfortably as many of my university students. I wanted to find out how that happened.

To my adoptive parents, my love for school, for university, for learning had always been an enigma. Even my mother, who was a schoolteacher, could not understand my drive to continue my education, first for a B.A., then a B.Ed., then an M.Ed., and finally the Ph.D., all done with no familial encouragement and with considerable sacrifice of time with my son and of money. My mother thought that when I met my blood family, I would discover the roots of this—to her, unusual—behavior. During the gathering at Michael's, I had asked each of my siblings what they had enjoyed most about school. "Nothing" was the most common reply. Michael had completed grade twelve general; Jackie, grade twelve commercial; a couple of them had stuck it out to the end of the eleventh grade; and the rest had dropped out sometime earlier in their high school days. None of them had liked school. None of them particularly liked to read and write beyond the necessities of their jobs and domestic life. I have to wonder whether the same would have been true for me had my adoptive mother not read to me from the time I was three and a half and had she not urged me to write about my experiences from the time I was eight. Was that early reading and writing the key to my success with and enjoyment of literacy activities? Is literacy development as simple and straightforward as that? And then, when I began to receive the letters from Jack Fleming, I saw another possibility. Despite the brevity of his formal education, he was indeed literate and could write not just interesting letters, but a vivid, dramatic, and sensitive narrative of his life. What's more, until he stopped, he had seemed to enjoy doing it. Is the connection between Jack's love of writing and my love of writing genetic? or is it that we both have something to write about, have a need to write about it, and know someone will be interested in reading it? And there is, in my case, the additional factor of my mother's encouraging me to write.

The word *intelligence* is bandied about extensively as a quantitative and therefore quantifiable entity. That a connection exists between what we call intelligence and what we call literacy seems axiomatic, and yet our understanding of the nature of that connection is tenuous. Intelligence is often assumed to involve the genetic programming that enables us to take advantage of the contexts of literacy potential that we encounter. More simply, if we are bright, we'll readily learn to read the print that surrounds us if indeed we are surrounded by print and encouraged to read it. These are such problematic assumptions and concepts that I hardly know where to begin unpacking them. How do we get to be bright? How do we get to be literate? Is it the same question?

I decided that if I could find out the answers to how my father had become such a fluent writer and how I had come to be perceived as bright and literate in the face of such dubious early projections, my story might have implications for other children predicted to fail; for parents planning to adopt older, neglected children; for social workers and caregivers working with unhappy, abused children, for all who decide later in life that they will not define their abilities according to limitations placed on them by others. And so I vowed I would visit my father, Jack Fleming.

JANUARY 30, 1994. CALGARY, ALBERTA. IT WOULD HAVE BEEN my twenty-ninth wedding anniversary had I still been married. Instead, it marks the first time in forty-nine years that my father and I will be together. With one light suitcase, I am first through customs and immediately recognize the tall gentleman with a slight limp, walking with a cane, as the person who must be my father. The three days I spend in his home reveal a life of physical and emotional hardships and challenges that seem beyond endurance. Jack Fleming is a storyteller, a true raconteur who takes delight in creating images to bring his tales to life. I see his brutal father, eating bacon, eggs, and toast for breakfast while his weary wife and thirteen children make do with bread dipped in pig lard flavored with sugar or coffee grounds. I see the sixteen-year-old Jack rented out by his father to a nearby farmer for forced labor, slipping on the manure-mired sapling floor of the barn, trying to harness a plow team with worn tack mended with barbed wire. I see Irene, my mother, as a vivacious, flirtatious, emotionally starved young woman, a lovely predator in a huge wide-brimmed black hat, dark hair, pale eyes, red lips, stealing the heart of my father. While their wedding guests were still partying, they had each slapped the other on the dance floor, argued, and left the reception separately, going to separate beds in separate living quarters. That fiery start continued throughout the short marriage. At their divorce, three years later, when the judge asked, "Did you cohabit with the two men named in the petition?" Irene replied with a laugh and a sneer, "Sure, and a couple hundred others." I realize that only one person's set of images are being put before me, and I work hard to understand that young woman who spent several years of her young life in a convent, who bore twelve babies, who neglected the ten that survived, who told her young husband, "You married me, not my body. My body is mine, and I will do with it what I please," whose credo, according to Jack, was, "You really never know a man until you sleep with him," and apparently she knew many.

And then I meet Marie, Jack's sister, who gasps when I enter her home, puts her hand to her throat, and says, "My God, it's like fifty years have rolled back, and Irene is walking into my front door. My girl, I held you in my arms when you were just a baby." So had Jack, and, for some reason that is the dominant image I take away from this three-day meeting. There are people alive who had held me with love as a baby.

What do I learn about literacy from that trip? Reading has been Jack's solace throughout his life, right from the first book he opened in the little village school in Plum Coulee. I have to surmise that so much reading transferred into a confidence and fluency in his writing. Jack offered no explanation, but he did let me know why he stopped his lengthy letters. His bone marrow has stopped producing new blood, and he requires regular transfusions. Writing saps his dwindling energy. There will be no more lengthy letters.

11

Through the Hawsehole to the Professoriate

I'LL NEVER BE SUSIE AGAIN

The increase in universal literacy did not bring about either general-ized highly specialized literate capabilities, or, and this is more significant, any marked decline in the general level of competence, no matter what the doubting say. Teachers will still be at the heart of the matter.

—M. Meek, *On Being Literate*, 208

ames Britton asserts that "how we teach is who we are." If teachers are, as Margaret Meek suggests, "at the heart of the matter" in the struggle toward universal literacy at the national and global levels, then who we are is critical to the kind of literacy teaching we will do, and to the kind of literacy learning that will occur in our classrooms. If we believe George Eliot's observation in *Middlemarch* that "we are all of us born in moral stupidity, taking the world as an udder to feed our supreme selves," then examining our own processes of emerging from this "moral stupidity" to moral awareness is one significant feature of becoming a more effective guide to those who depend upon our counsel and instruction. Although it was not a conscious intention at the outset, one major strand of this literacy narrative has disclosed some specific correlations between my literacy experiences and the slow evolution of my moral awareness. This chapter extends that development to teaching and learning.

IN A FOXHOLE IN WAR-TORN FRANCE, TWO SOLDIERS TALKED about their lives, their loves, their ambitions, their hopes, but rarely their fears. They did not talk about language. They survived, parted ways, and spent much of their subsequent lives talking and writing and teaching about language, one in the United States, the other in England. When their paths crossed again, many years after World War II, it was at an international conference of language scholars. Their wartime camaraderie renewed itself as academic collegiality and high respect for each other's work. It was consequently fitting for Wayne Booth, of the University of Chicago, to serve as honored guest speaker at Harold Rosen's retirement from the University of London.

Booth strode to the podium with silver-haired splendor, his tall frame radiating confidence, and hit me square in my imposter syndrome. Booth called it hypocrisy, and he legitimized it as a necessary and appropriate transition stage in learning how to be. It was a lesson I found enormously useful in becoming part of the professoriate in American higher education.

The notion is simple, as many profound insights into the complexity of human behavior are. Whenever we take on a new role, for example becoming a professor of English, we first act out that role. Based on our understanding and our observations of how people in that role represent themselves to their colleagues and to their students, we select characteristics that match the values we have or hope to have and then act out a version of how we think an English professor behaves. We are impostors or hypocrites. At first, we are terrified of being "found out," of being unmasked and having our true inadequacies revealed, but then as day after day goes by, the values and characteristics we act out become part of who we really are. Amazingly, hypocrisy becomes integrity.

An unexpected retirement at my alma mater, the Faculty of Education at the University of Manitoba, opens up a one-year assistant professorship in elementary English education. Because of my familiarity with the faculty and the system, it would be a smooth orientation to university teaching for me. But elementary education is not my major area of expertise, so I accept a position for which I am more directly qualified, in the English department at Indiana University–Purdue University at Indianapolis (IUPUI).

Wayne Booth's concept of transition from hypocrisy to integrity sustains me as I begin to teach writing on the urban commuter campus of an American university. Although credentially qualified through my doctoral studies of writing and through my experience as an English teacher, I have never actually taken a writing class in my school or university career. My first class is what is politely called a developmental class, which means that the students have little fluency and even less confidence or competence in their writing skills. Looking at the writing done by these students, who range from fresh-faced eighteen-year-olds to work-weary fiftysomething, I realize I have several options. I can play the role of superteacher and take on the tremendous challenge of trying to "fix all the faults" in their writing and get them ready for regular college writing; I can play gatekeeper and separate those likely to succeed from those unlikely to succeed and concentrate my efforts on the ones most likely to make it to the next course; I can play nurturer and try to help everyone in class feel better about their writing, so that at least they will develop some confidence in their ability to demonstrate their thinking and learning in writing; I can play servicer to the university, and focus my attention on those writing skills deemed crucial to at least minimal success in the academy; I can play guardian of ethics and advise the weakest that they should withdraw, pick up their refund, and enter the world of work; I can play ingenue and just jump in and dog-paddle through the challenges on an ad hoc intuitive basis. What is my responsibility to my students, who for various reasons see a university education as their means to a more rewarding life; to my university, whose mission to the community includes educating—not just awarding degrees to—nontraditional students nontraditionally prepared; to my ingrained concept of the university as a site of intellectual rigor and striving for excellence; to myself beginning the process of entering the professoriate?

Being able to articulate options is a necessary prelude to learning. I realize that my developmental students and I have a lot in common. We are both in strange territory and both learning how to present ourselves appropriately in that territory, they as scholar-learners and I as a scholar-teacher. As I have to select appropriate values and behaviors to fill the role of learned professor, they have to determine appropriate values and behaviors to become intellectually motivated university students. What better than to learn these roles together? And so I turn my smorgasbord of choices over to my students, and together we mull through them. Then we work at articulating their options, and within a couple of class periods, we are all hard at work in the process of becoming what we want to become in American higher education.

Possibly because I had also been a nontraditional student at university, prior to the term even having been coined, I am able to identify and work with the similarities between my students as learners and me as professor-learner. I keep thinking of the description of William Bligh in *Mutiny on the Bounty*: he had been no gentleman born to the captaincy; he had crawled up through the hawsehole, the hawsehole being the name of the opening up from the common sailors' quarters. It seems to me, during these first years of university teaching, that my students and I are both crawling up through the hawsehole, out from the present circumstances of our lives and toward the making of better circumstances.

Meanwhile, as a Canadian in the United States, I am also contending with culture shock, made even more pronounced by my recent three years in London. Just a glance at an ordinary academic day as I experienced it in each country will highlight some of the differences. In Britain it had been difficult to locate a lecturer or reader (there was only one faculty member per department who merited the title "professor") before ten o'clock; impossible before nine. In Canada, at eight o'clock, I was often the earliest to arrive, but by eight-thirty, coffee, conversation, and classes or desk work were well under way. At IUPUI, by eight o'clock, every spot in the nearest parking lots is already taken. In England everything stopped for elevenses: coffee, conversation, and a sticky bun. Then lunch and conversation at one o'clock in the Common Room, tea and conversation at four, again in the Common Room, and a comfortable leaving time between five and six unless there was an evening class to teach. Manitoba was almost the same, but without the sticky bun. Morning coffee, lunch, and afternoon tea were social breaks in the professional day and were enjoyed in the company of colleagues. At IUPUI the most common social opportunity is a brown bag lunch meeting to talk about professional concerns. Otherwise, coffee is a quick grab-and-gulp in the office, lunch is eaten with one hand while grading papers or turning the pages of a recent journal article with the other, and tea time is unheard-of. Evenings are for working; weekends are for working; vacation time is for doing research, writing books or articles, or teaching summer school. The pace is frenetic.

Even worse, I become used to it, to the extent that if a colleague or student drops into my office unexpectedly for a chat, I almost shoo them out, and definitely signal my impatience to get back to my "real" work of preparing for class, grading papers, or writing papers. One day I drop in on a colleague to chat about something that is important to me, and see the same worried furrows on her brow that I always feel on mine when my time is interrupted. I excuse myself as quickly as I can, leave my work-cluttered office, and take a long, thoughtful walk along the nearby canal that is just being developed in downtown Indianapolis. I deliberately walk slowly—something that is very difficult for me—and force myself to look at every tree, every shrub, and most important, every human being that I pass. I keep saying to myself, "People are more important than paperwork."

I then adapt the British university tradition of "sporting the oak"—a two-door system of letting people know whether you are willing to receive visitors—to my single-door office. If I am in my office but absolutely too busy for unscheduled visits or interruptions, I close my door. If I am very busy but available if needed, I crack my door open just an inch or two. If I am just regularly busy, I leave my door wide open, welcoming any student or colleague who wants to visit for a moment or a while. Amazingly, without any explanation, the system works.

At the end of my first year in Indianapolis, an invitation arrives for the twenty-fifth reunion of Manitoba Teachers College Class of 1963. I decide not to go. Then the telephone rings.

"Hello, Susie?"

Susie! My name from the past; a voice from the past. It is Ed Toews from Teachers College, who had flirted both guilelessly and guilefully with me and with almost every other female at the college. Handsome, rowdy, friendly, always-with-a-ready-smile Eddy Toews. I had been afraid to date him at Teachers College, alarmed by his roisterous sexuality. He has recently joined the faculty at Bruns, the school I had left four years earlier to go to London, as a physical education teacher, and he has tracked me down through the Faculty of Education to my new position in Indianapolis. He wants me to accompany him to the reunion.

"Sure," I reply on impulse, throwing out my resolution not to go. At the reunion I am suffocated by my own creation. Twenty-five years earlier, not wanting to be at Teachers College, I had created another persona, a kind of alter ego, and named her Susie, the name my brother and father had called me interchangeably with Floozie. Susie was, in essence, a bit of a floozie. She was glamorous in the cheap kind of way that someone unaccustomed to glamor envisions it. She was confident, bordering on brassy and sassy, and a definite anti-intellectual. When she ran (and lost) for secretary of the Student Council, a job she had already capably performed in an interim capacity during the six-week beginning of term before the elections took place, her publicity badges were heart-shaped and read, deliberately provocatively, "Susie for Sec." Few of the really nice young women liked Susie, except those able to see the vulnerability behind her mask. The older women were different. They seemed to have antennae to who and what Susie really was, and they had been more friendly.

Having been asked by the reunion committee, as soon as they found out I was planning to come, to deliver a summary retrospective of that year so long ago, I try to present myself in true Wayne Boothian fashion as a serious professional able to sprinkle humor throughout a competently delivered talk. It is how I want to see myself evolving. The surprised appreciation of my former college mates signals immediately that this is not how they had anticipated I would evolve. We all form images of how we think some people will live out their lives, and it is a shock when these people deviate from our expectations. I feel the weight of their expectations that I would continue my frivolous superficiality right into old age.

Though during the afternoon and early part of the evening I struggle against my classmates' reactions to me as Susie, I eventually succumb. Of course, having arrived with the most notorious womanizer of the class of 1963, I have whetted their appetite for the slaughter of this new, supposedly more dignified, persona of "the professor" right from the start. And there is still the devil inside me who delights in knocking people's expectations off balance, so I deliberately play along with the jokes and comments. By ten o'clock, I am mired in Susie quicksand. I have been trapped, in Proustian fashion, by accepting and then rendering other people's definitions of who and what I am, based ironically on a definition of a persona that I had deliberately manufactured and that I thought had been discarded years ago. Sitting on a table, surrounded by a dozen of my classmates of 1963, I have taken the center of attention, telling slightly risqué stories and jokes, laughing and flirting. I wouldn't mind so much—in fact, part of me kind of likes Susie's guileless openness—except that I cannot, despite many energetic attempts, elevate the tone of that scene beyond that early sixties silliness. Susie and her friends maintain their hold on the tone that has been set, and I cannot escape it. I want to talk to these people about their evolution as teachers and learners over the past twenty-five years, but Susie and her friends just want to laugh and play. I feel smothered. I am living out Kurt Vonnegut's corollary to Wayne Booth's theory of hypocrisy: "We are what we pretend to be, so we must be careful what we pretend to be."

It becomes one of those scenes that in subsequent months plays itself over and over again in my mind, forcing reflection and response. At the same time, there seems to be something inescapably self-indulgent in fretting about the interior landscape of my mind and soul when the various exterior landscapes of the world are so fraught with tension and challenge. I don't know how to get around that, how to find an appropriate balance between solving the tensions of my inner world and following my social and professional responsibilities concerning tensions in the external world. I do, however, think there is a correlation between the two. I know that I usually feel better positioned to attend to societal problems after I have made secure steps in resolving my own problems. I also know that my students face similar tensions and that our in-class engagements with literacy—reading about others' encounters with internal and external problems and writing about our own internal and external worlds—contribute to the resolution of these tensions at the personal level.

These basic acts of literacy—writing about one's turmoil and reading about the turmoil of others—have the potential to move us into and beyond our own personal resolutions. I referred earlier to C. S. Lewis' student's remark in *Shadowlands* that "we read to know we are not alone." In *Women Who Run with the Wolves*, Clarissa Pinkola Estes reminds us that long ago *alone* used to be treated as two words: *all one*, meaning wholly one, complete within oneself. We read, then, to know that we are not all one, that our struggles mirror the struggles of humanity; our hopes and fears are microcosms of everyone's hopes and fears.

That thought motivates me to return to the passage in Proust that had stimulated my thinking about how we may shape ourselves according to others' perceptions of who we are and how we should behave and what we should achieve. Proust expresses it this way:

> Our social personality is created by the thoughts of other people. Even the simple act we describe as "seeing someone we know" is, to some extent, an intellectual process. We pack the physical outline of the creature we see with all of the ideas we have already formed about him. . . . In the end they come to fill out so completely the curve of his cheeks, to follow so exactly the line of his nose, they blend so harmoniously in the sound of his voice that these seem to be no more than a transparent envelope, so that each time we see the face or hear the voice it is our own ideas of him which we recognize and to which we listen.

In the interim between first reading that passage in 1983 and trying to locate it again several years later for this book, I had reformed the image of a transparent envelope into a much more horrible one: While envisioning myself as the totality of others' perceptions of me within a transparent skin, I had imagined a huge and ugly insectlike creature with black and brown twists and curves packed inside a tightly stretched clear shell as the representative icon of this remembered concept. It was clearly how I had perceived the way others perceived me. After rereading the original passage, I realize that it is now clearly time to reformulate that image into something more respectful not only of myself but also of those whose lives intersect with mine.

We write, in part, to arrive at our own resolutions of turmoil, and we discover that our personal resolutions may extend outward to resolutions of larger parts of society. A case in point might be this book. Writing it has already contributed to my own deeper understanding of myself, my family, my students, and my work at the university. If one person reading it comes away with a more positive attitude toward children who have been prematurely labeled uneducable or socially inept, and that person understands the role that reading and writing can play in helping children envision possible worlds beyond their immediate environment, then this book will have gone beyond my own immediate ability to contribute to the lives of these children. Multiply that extension by ten or twenty, and the possibilities for a personal act of self-understanding to influence other people become almost boundless.

In this manner, I justify the pursuit of balance in my interior landscape as a necessary prelude to my understanding how to explore and contribute to resolving tensions of the exterior world. In the days, weeks, and months following the reunion, that Susie-mired scene replays itself. I decide to respond to the challenge in the same way that I advise my students to respond to similar personal tensions and in the way that my mother advised me to deal with my emotional tensions while I was growing up: I decide to write about it.

EPILOGUE

Tracings from the Wild Ones

SO WHAT? WHO CARES?

Narratives are one sort of trace that we leave in the world. All our

literatures are leavings, of the same order as the myths of wilderness

peoples who leave behind only stories and a few stone tools.

—Gary Snyder, *"Nature's Writing,"* unpublished

NARRATIVE TRACINGS ESTABLISH THE HISTORY AND POWER OF literacy. Our journals, essays, stories, and poems are the lettered walls of our cave, reflecting only schematically and in dim light the fullness and complexity of our existence. Nonetheless, aware of the limitations of our scratchings, we persist. We need to lay down our life outside of us, in some form of tracing, in written text, in order to discover and understand the life essence inside of us. That is one reason for the creation of this book.

But there is another reason, less egocentric in its motivation. Roughly a quarter of a century ago I came across a poem by Stephen Spender, "An Elementary School Classroom in a Slum," a poem that stirred me—and continues to stir me—to a more profound realization of my responsibilities as an educator, a parent, and a writer. Writers create their tracings, among other impulses, to be read. Reading other people's tracings—poems, novels, biographies, plays—has enabled me first to imagine beyond and then to reach beyond my immediate grasp, thereby eventually to grasp what seemed originally beyond my reach. And so I hope that what I write in this narrative will help those who work and play with children—as teachers, parents, caregivers, counselors—to believe in their charges' ability to reach beyond their immediately perceivable grasp. Spender addresses this hope, this responsibility, directly:

> Unless, governor, teacher, inspector, visitor,
> This map becomes their window and these windows
> That shut upon their lives like catacombs,
> Break O break open until they break the town
> And show the children to green fields, and make their world
> Run azure on gold sands, and let their tongues
> Run naked into books, the white and green leaves open
> History theirs whose language is the sun.

But writing and reading are not to be solitary ventures; they are to be shared, discussed, questioned, and elaborated upon among friends, family, and colleagues. Margaret Meek highlights the significance of conversation about what we read and what we write in relation to our literacy development:

> Come then. What is it to be literate? We have to draw our own maps, trace our own histories, acknowledge our own debts and consider ways not taken. Our literacy autobiographies reveal riches and gaps, but these narratives are not tales of solitary journeys. We were always in dialogue with others—those who taught us to read, those for whom we wrote, who lent us books, shaped our preferences, encouraged us, forbade us even. They were dead poets, living authors, cynical critics. We remember them as friends who made our world more habitable, who helped us, as we read and wrote, to discover who we were and who we could become. (*On Being Literate*, 234)

Those of us who leave traces for others to follow and interpret, and those of us who follow and interpret these tracings, and those of us who explore our interpretations in dialogue with others: we are all wild ones in Gary Snyder's sense of *wild*, "a name for the way that phenomena continually actualize themselves. . . ." We forage in our own wildernesses to write for ourselves, for each other, and for anyone else who cares to follow our traces. We forage in the wildernesses of others as we read and, for a while, live the lives of others. As we talk about these readings and writings with our fellow sojourners, we forge our understanding of and role in the civilized world we inhabit on a daily basis. We are, to apply Snyder's view of natural phenomena, literally actualizing ourselves—making ourselves, our experiences, our thoughts, our ways of observing and interpreting the world, actual—through our reading and our writing.

The process of writing this book has become an integral part of the process of teaching, learning, and writing in my classes. As I read my students' forays into their wildernesses, they read mine. It is an open invitation for my students to see that literacy, that writing—others' as well as their own— is a way to understand not just their positions and perspectives in their world but also how and why they have arrived at those positions and perspectives, and why and how they might wish to maintain them or to change them. It may provide, for some, a small flame of inspiration to see that the gap between the lives they lead and the lives they want to lead is surmountable. The gap can be crossed, and literacy is one means of enabling this to happen.

Writing about our own histories and the role that literacy has played in our evolution of self leads beyond a deeper understanding of self to an understanding and acceptance of those whose lives have intersected with ours. I wanted, in particular, those students who had motivated me to write this story—Angie Martin, Stephanie Rodriguez, and Ann Nicholas— to respond to it in relation to their own literate lives, and in relation to their individual attempts to negotiate the gap between the lives they led and the lives they hoped to lead. Angie couldn't do it. Soon after her divorce from a husband who beat her and made her feel substandard and inadequate, she remarried, this time to a man who has forbidden her access to anything related to the university. Ann, now teaching in a small rural school while coming to terms with multiple sclerosis, poured onto paper the sea change between her view of the world a half dozen years ago and her current view. She begins:

> It is a sentimental sport of sorts to call upon past images. I shudder when I recall the noble picture I had of myself. The transformation came on its own, back behind me, as though I had walked into an amusement park fun house. There is no sad story within my life. On the contrary, I believed I was normal. That is the same amusement park fun house magic that has continually distorted my thinking. I have had two failed marriages and three children. The youngest lives with her father "for her own good." I get her as often as possible.

Ann goes on to describe the "wilderness" of her young adulthood, the agony of losing custody of her youngest child through false allegations of child abuse, and the challenges of beginning a teaching career after turning to formal education as the means of crossing the gap between the life she was living and the life she aspired to. She concludes with the following insights into her own relationships between literacy and teaching:

> I am teaching students that other teachers have given up on. But it is worth it to me when I can see their positive, talented side and I can see an improvement. So, am I the type of teacher I am becoming through my education or because of my experiences? I like to think that I get and give from both. After all, how could I ever have loved Homer's epics as the massive adventures that they are without my drive for the thrill of the ultimate adventure myself? How could I teach my students about the ups and downs of the human condition in Stephen Crane's "The Open Boat" if I had never felt those same emotions? How could I help my students understand the tragedy of a family lost in a father's old-fashioned ideas of being a successful provider in Arthur Miller's *Death of a Salesman* if I had not known the hurt and humiliation of failure? The connections are endless. But there are new emotions and ideas that I have not yet experienced to be learned as well. There's James Fenimore Cooper's *The Deerslayer* for learning the challenges of another home and culture, for just one example. . . . Yes, my reading affects my outlook on life just as much as my outlook on life affects my reading.

And finally, Stephanie describes how, rather than helping her cross the gap, increased awareness through literacy almost caused her to give up in despair. She frames her response in the following writing as an answer to the two questions I ask my students to consider before handing in their final drafts: So what? Who cares?

> Reading was not generally encouraged in my childhood, and by the time I officially dropped out of school on my sixteenth birthday I was much more familiar with *Green Acres* than with *Green Gables*.
>
> My return to school was both good and bad. Surprised at the number of things I didn't know and was eager to learn, I set out to seek "The Truth."
>
> Of course it began with guided reading, and at first it was wonderful. Freud and Plato did their parts to help me progress in my personal life. I stopped smoking, lost forty pounds, and began to understand my children. I perceived myself as becoming a better person. Life was good. But I kept reading, and the inevitable happened. I came, for the first time, in intellectual contact with the others—with "them."
>
> Malthus started it. He said that I was nothing but an ill effect of society. Spencer backed him up completely adding that, according to the laws of nature, my children and I didn't deserve to live. We were unfit,

me and mine. Social Darwinism denied us the right to exist. We were poor. Always had been. But now I realized what that must mean to people who weren't poor—the others. I realized what our condition told them about us. The world quickly divided into "us" and "them," and I was ashamed to be a member of "us." "The Truth" had not set me free.

Everything changed. Life became worse than it had ever been before I came to school, before I knew.

Oh, it was the same bus I got off at night, the same street that I dragged myself down, the same bookbag over my shoulder. But it looked different now. Now, the shopping bag that I carried with just enough groceries for one day wasn't something to be grateful for but merely an example of the inefficiency of poverty. I could see no hope of significant change, for I knew, now, how this had come to be and what it meant.

I began to dislike looking at my children; their futures were no brighter than my own. I lost my pride in them; they existed merely out of the generosity of their betters. They, in turn, gradually began to look at me differently. Perhaps "The Truth" showed in my face.

Cruelty became understandable to me. Nothing I heard on the news shocked me anymore. Hell, ninety percent of all the species ever on Earth are extinct now, wiped out through natural selection. If nature doesn't have respect for life, why should we? "The Truth" was making me sick.

Writing was better. Writing about my experiences made them different somehow, less threatening, not so scary. I became able to pull a situation from my memory, even a horrible situation and, on paper, render it powerless to hurt me anymore. I could tell of my father's death, my husband's abuses, my own ignorance, whatever I wanted, and in the telling make it seem not quite so bad. My father, my husband, my self all became characters in a story. A story that I could look at from a distance. A story that made more and more sense as I read it again and again, told each time from a new angle or with some different focus.

The new peace that came with understanding myself did not disturb my sense of "us" and "them." And I must confess here, Dr. Hamilton, that I clearly perceived you (and most faculty) as "them."

I feel it important that you get to know a little bit of my house before I respond to *My Name's not Susie*. The following is a brief account of a tiny part of the day that you gave me the manuscript to read. I still have my kids—today.

They're there. I can hear them as I approach the front door.

"Bitch!"

"Bastard!"

Not the typical sounds of children at play. Their voices slow my step. I get closer; the voices get louder, my pace even slower. The door opens and I freeze. They haven't seen me yet and I think for an instant of running. Just drop the bags, the milk, the responsibility, and run, run forever. I know that I won't though. Not today.

Later I sit at one of the two chairs pulled up to the table and around me they crowd.

"Mommie," in a half dozen voices at once, followed by the rush:

"Shut up, Nessie. I was talking."

"I was talking to her first."

"No you weren't, you stupid little brat!"

"Mom, I'm kicking Jorgie's butt."

"No, you knew I was gonna tell her something."

"Rude pig!"

"Pee pants!"

"Mom!"

I look for a second into each face as it speaks. I can't keep up, and finally stare into the pot of beans and weenies on the table and only vaguely consider strategies for gaining control.

"Time out!" I force my voice.

I wish they didn't stop so quickly. I wish they didn't all look directly at me waiting, questioning, . . . needing.

"What?" Nessie breaks the silence.

I look again into each face, each pair of eyes, back at the beans and weenies.

"I don't know," I whisper, really not knowing. "Let's just eat."

Earlier that day a friend of mine had suggested that the time I'd spent getting an education was a waste because school was useless to people like "us." Right about then I believed that very much. School seemed pretty damned useless in my dining room every night. Those things benefited only "them"; they who were smart enough to have never gotten into a hopeless situation like mine. They who'd had guidance, and money, and everything set out for them from the beginning. They who couldn't help but succeed. Maybe I would fare better with a job at the Seven-Eleven than with a college degree.

This was the setting in which I began reading your book. I met in this book a person that I already knew, Dr. Hamilton, nice enough, but worldly, scholarly, impressive even among "them." To view this respected figure as a problematic little girl in an orphanage, dirty, unpromising, unwanted was, to say the least, an eye-opening experience. I was at first shocked, then intrigued, and finally and lastingly, inspired.

I don't know if the wall that I created between "them" and "us" will ever fall down, but it has certainly been weakened here.

I don't know if I'll ever get where you are, but knowing you were once where I am makes it seem possible. Maybe I won't get as far as you are, but I know that the wall is scalable. I feel hope, for myself and for my children.

You mention in your book that your students are free to call you Sharon but that many choose to call you Dr. Hamilton. In the past, I chose to call you Dr. Hamilton out of respect for our differences. It is with a sense of pride in our similarities that I will continue to address you as Dr. Hamilton.

You ask, "So what? Who cares?"

I do.

Bibliography

Eliot, George. 1964. *Middlemarch.* New York: NAL-Dutton.

Eliot, T.S. 1971. *East Coker.* Boston: Faber and Faber Ltd.

Eliot, T.S. 1976. *Love Song of J. Alfred Prufrock.* Mattituck: Amereon Ltd.

Meek, Margaret. 1992. *On Being Literate.* Portsmouth: Heinemann.

Proust, Marcel. *Remembrance of Things Past.* New York: Random House, Inc.

Spender, Stephen. 1970. *Selected Poems.* New York: Random House, Inc.